PROG ROCK DOWN-UNDER

Disclaimer:
All opinions expressed in this book represent the opinions of the author only. All information is believed to be factually accurate at time of writing. No attempt is made to offer a complete history or discography of any artist(s) included in this book.

Logue, Colin (author)
PROG ROCK DOWN-UNDER
ISBN: 978-1-922890-13-9
Music | Short Stories

Minion Pro 10.5pt/14pt
Book design by Green Hill Publishing

PROG ROCK DOWN-UNDER

COLIN LOGUE

contents

August 4th 2019. With Dad to celebrate his 93rd birthday.

Dedicated to the memories of:

Ian Alexander Logue
4/8/1926 – 7/2/2021
Dad and much more. Will be sorely missed.

Thomas Samuel Logue
Died suddenly 28/12/2021
Uncle Sammy – my favourite uncle

And

Elayne Bechaz
(31/1/1956 – 10/7/2021)
Wonderful mother and grandmother of our family

Grateful thanks and love to my beautiful wife **Louise.**
Family and **friends** for amazing support.
All **the musicians** who selflessly gave their time
and encouragement.

You have all added to this journey called 'life'.

PReFace

PROGRESSIVE ROCK AND AUSTRALIA would, on the face of it, appear to be strange bed-fellows. Australia is more renowned for 'pub-rock' with bands such as; *The Angels, Cold Chisel* and *Midnight Oil* among the leading proponents.

Progressive rock (prog) had its birth primarily in the UK and Europe before breaking through in the United States of America. Australia followed but did not receive the media attention or acclaim that was enjoyed by the pioneers of the genre in Europe and England in particular.

The continuing reluctance of the media – both print and radio – to extend time and space to the genre is regrettable and most modern Australian prog bands have made Europe a 'second home' as the market is much more accommodating, with opportunities to perform live to receptive (and large) audiences more prevalent.

The *Australian Pink Floyd Show*, who had their birth in Adelaide, struggled to gain any sizeable foothold in their home country but the UK and Europe have taken to them to such an extent that they now tour extensively in the northern hemisphere and rarely, if at all, perform in Australia.

In the twenty-first century progressive rock is enjoying a resurgence world-wide and Australia has contributed with some excellent bands producing music to enhance the genre.

My purpose is to present some of the artists and, hopefully, entice you to consider their work in a more favourable light.

The opinions expressed within these pages are not intended to form an authoritative view but are, purely, my own opinions.

INTRODUCTION

WHEN I ARRIVED IN Australia (1987) I found the lack of a 'prog scene' both puzzling and annoying, after-all I had come from the northern hemisphere where the genre was still revered and enjoying a resurgence through the so-called 'neo-prog' movement with *Marillion, IQ, Pallas* and *Twelfth Night* leading the way.

The vast majority of music journalists and pundits in Australia seldom (never, in my experience) seem to mention Australian progressive rock or extol any of the fine musicians and bands who have represented the genre over the last fifty years or so.

During my time with the Australian Broadcasting Corporation we received a questionnaire regarding musical content. I suggested that the progressive rock genre was sadly overlooked and perhaps this could be considered more favourably by programmers and list-setters. The response was – more-or-less – predictable. The ABC had a certain demographic in mind when considering the type of music which it was willing to broadcast. That demographic, they determined, would not be those who would appreciate 'this' type of music. Probing further into this 'demographic' led to the answer that the general age group – at the time – of ABC listeners was thirty-five to sixty therefore musical content needed to reflect and cater for this group. At the time I was approaching fifty years of age and had been listening to progressive rock for over thirty years. My considered opinion was that the demographic the ABC was endeavouring to reach would have grown up with this genre and many would have appreciated the musical ability of the artists. Sadly, my arguments fell on deaf ears.

It, therefore, came as quite a surprise to discover that the ABC youth station, triple j, included *Anubis* in its 'unearthed' series – CDs issued to promote new and/or unsigned artists (a precursor of sorts to the CD giveaways now popular with glossy music magazines). The resulting entry on 'google' is effusive in its praise of the band and contains good data on band members and their debut album.

During the global pandemic of 2020 the Australian progressive rock band, *Caligula's Horse*, released the album *'Rise Radiant'* which received glowing reviews in Europe and America. As the band was unable to tour they decided to work on the album and release it during this time as a 'thank you' to their fans. The release was ignored – in the main – by mainstream media and press in Australia. Surprised? I'm not. It is this reason and many other typical examples that prompted me to write about the growing and exemplary progressive rock movement in Australia.

This book will not be exhaustive and will be no means cover the many artists aligning themselves to the genre in Australia. My criteria was to highlight those which I have embraced personally and present short essays (by way of introduction) to inform and enlighten the 'prog-starved' Australian public and, by extension, a wider audience.

Progressive rock has always been the 'poor relation' but consider this, during the 'halcyon years' of the early seventies many progressive bands sold millions of albums world-wide, touring to arena-sized audiences and filled the music press pages with their latest release or tour.

It is true the genre suffered a decline but contrary to popular myth it never faded away or died with the advent of punk – or any other popular genre. The fact that many of those early pioneers still tour, record and release new material should be ample evidence of the enduring appeal of progressive rock.

I invite you into the world of progressive music by way of the Australian bands who continue to represent the genre in the twenty-first century but who are, by and large, over-looked in their own 'backyard'.

What progressive rock is (or isn't) is akin to opening the proverbial 'can of worms' and not within the parameters of this book. Ask twenty 'prog' fans and receive twenty conflicting answers.

My advice is simple. If you enjoy it then that is more than enough and I invite you to enjoy and sample some of Australia's best.

I would like to take this opportunity to thank some of the people who extended a 'helping hand' by way of 'subjecting' themselves to my questions:

- *David Eaton*
  (Anubis)
- *Sam Vallen*
  (Caligula's Horse)
- *Simon Wood* and *Colin Andrews*
  (Kettlespider/Malcura)
- *Geoff Dawes*
  (Merlin Bird)
- *Mark Trueack*
  (Unitopia/United Progressive Fraternity)

Thank you for your kind words of encouragement and generously giving your time to indulge me.

anubis

ANUBIS FIRST CAME TO my attention through the pages of the UK magazine 'Prog' with their excellent album *Hitchhiking to Byzantium* (2014). That is a sad indictment of Australia's music media.

A few years later I found their website and on seeing a 'special offer' to purchase their entire catalogue - six studio albums and one live album – for a very reasonable price - the decision was a 'no-brainer'.

Anubis is often described as a 'cinematic progressive rock band'. In itself that description indicates that their music is expansive and, to some degree, symphonic. I find it impossible to argue with the 'perceived' descriptor and, in fact *David Eaton* (keyboards, guitar and founding member) is more than pleased to embrace it. He informed me, "That's our strength – we like the music to convey the story as much as the lyrics"

Anubis are primarily a Sydney based band and formed in 2004 around the nucleus of *Robert James Moulding* (vocals/guitar/bass) and *David Eaton* (keyboards). This partnership decided to produce a concept album which would honour their departed friend – who would remain anonymous. The result was their debut album *230503* (2008).

The album has extensive linear notes by *David Eaton* and the title is reference to the date when they were informed about a mutual friend who had disappeared during a boating trip. It was – according to *Eaton* – "never meant to be anyone's first album". The person in question has since been identified as '*Evan McGee*' but the album is not directly about him – *Eaton* considered this to be disrespectful to the family.

230503 is an expansive and cinematic experience which mines the progressive rock genre to the full. It does not mimic or any way set out to copy what has gone before but delivers a whole new feel to a tried and trusted formula – if that is not a contradiction in terms within the genre.

The nucleus of the band was extended by the addition of *Steven Eaton* (drums/percussion) and *Douglas Skene* (guitars), with others lending support to various tracks, most notably *Dean Bennison*.

The Deepest Wound is the opening track and starts with effects which lead into superb vocal and guitar as track-by-track the seamless narrative unfolds. Given the basis of the album it is difficult not to be drawn into an almost melancholic feel.

Waterfall is enhanced by some incredible bass guitar – an instrument I have, unfortunately, both a fondness for and ineptitude with.

Anonymity is jarring and compelling in equal measure with a swirling conclusion, while *the bond of mutual distrust* continues in a similar vein.

By track seven *'the doctor'* we find ourselves in 'commercial rock' mode. This is followed by *flying/falling* which is keyboard dominated and leads into the two epic tracks which end the album.

The Collapse commences with a vocal refrain which is both piercing and evocative and is infused with atmospheric keyboards.

The album ends with *'disinfected and abused'* an epic which adheres to the 'prog epic' from any era of the genre. Swirling keyboards, confronting vocals and added saxophone bring this debut album to the dramatic conclusion it deserves with an almost 'Floydian' feel.

I was informed that *230503* will soon be re-issued with different linear notes and the version I own is now out of print. In answer to my question regarding quoting from the original *David* replied "Go right ahead. It'll be nice that they're available somehow"

By kind permission of *David Eaton* I will reproduce the first paragraph, which details the impetus behind the album.

"Unidentified male, 20 years old, frustrated in the lack of direction and meaning in his life leads to his searching for what he believes is missing. Confused by his shyness and naivety, he finally meets a girl on the internet, and shortly afterward leaves to be with her. After a romantic date on a houseboat he gives his lady a silver pendant, and, disguising the emotion, steps out for some air, in some sort of freak accident/misjudgement he disappears off the edge of the boat and is not seen again. Police helicopters circle, failing to detect anything. The dreadful news is duly delivered to his distraught family".

This opening paragraph to the extensive and informative linear notes offer an indication of how difficult it must have been to compose the album.

Further on *Eaton* details the making of the album and some of the problems incurred, which has probably prompted the re-issue. He states, "Nowadays, I tend to think *230503* suffered from some of the heavy-handed editing. A lot of really good stuff got omitted as a result of my rather misguided quest for perfection, which I heavily regret now".

The re-issue will be interesting, hearing just what is made of it, with new technology and a large dose of hindsight. I look forward to hearing the finished product – hopefully in the very near future.

David Eaton, Steve Eaton and *Robert (Rob) James Moulding* all attended the same school – albeit six years apart. *Eaton* also knew *Rob's* sister with whom he worked at a local pizza franchise during his university days.

Rob was playing with a punk band with political leanings which *David* describes as "awful". He did, however, think *Rob* had a great voice "even if it wasn't as refined as it became later". The two 'English boys in Australia' quickly formed a friendship and *Rob* was introduced to *Pink Floyd* and *Yes*. Being a bass 'picking' guitarist he, quiet naturally, fell under the spell of *Chris Squire (Yes)*.

The line-up expanded as their debut album began taking shape and recording got under way. Some decided not to play their chosen instrument with *David* (a guitarist) "It's my main instrument" concentrating on keyboards (which he had been playing for five years) as "keys players for prog bands don't come up very often in Sydney". *Rob* wanted to focus on vocals so another bass player was recruited – *Nicholas (Nick) Antoinette*, who remained in the band for the next three years.

Their next album would see some further fine-tuning to the line-up, now consisting of; *Robert James Moulding* (vocals/percussion/guitar), *David Eaton* (keyboards/vocals/guitar), *Douglas Skene* (guitars/vocals), *Dean Bennison* (steel guitar/clarinet/vocals), *Steven Eaton* (drums/percussion/vocals), *Nicholas Antoinette* (bass guitar/vocals) and *Martyn Cook* (flute/saxophone).

A Tower of Silence (2011) is in many ways a continuation – it is conceptual and cinematic – of their debut album and commences with the epic track *The Passing Bell (I–VI)*. I have always been a 'lover' of prog epics and this particular track is appealing. It is not overblown or bombastic but is captivating with drumming which both keeps the beat and adds atmosphere. The vocals have an almost, in my opinion, 'Bob Marley' feel but are definitely rock infused. It seamlessly melds into *Archway of Tears* before you realise it. *The Final Resting Place* is equally epic and strong in structure and musicality.

A Tower of Silence is a ghost story in the classic sense. An eleven year old girl's spirit is trapped in the walls of a Victorian workhouse where she worked and died. As the story progresses we discover just how she came to be trapped. Adventurous and ambitious this concept takes one on a journey through a compelling story enhanced by superb musicianship.

The final track (again an epic) *All That is* (in three parts) is a fitting conclusion and makes a mockery of the so-called 'second album syndrome'. I'm sure you are aware of the old chestnut 'it takes twenty years to compose your first album and six months to compose the next'.

This is where my personal introduction to Anubis enters the fray with the release of *Hitchhiking to Byzantium* (2014), through the pages of the UK magazine 'Prog'.

I have read reviews both extolling and decrying the album. Some believe it to be 'less-than-perfect' while others consider it a continuation of the band's development, stretching themselves musically. Why the widely differing opinions? What had Anubis done differently to attract such conflicting reviews?

What follows is my opinion of the album with a track-by-track analysis.

The album itself abandons the conceptual path for a more personal approach wherein each member of the band contributed lyrics based on their own life experiences.

Fadeout (a humorously odd title for an opening track) begins with an ethereal feel dominated by keyboards and percussion. It is relatively short before...fading out!

A King with no Crown has a 'busier' sound and again the percussion is a dominate force. *Robert Moulding'* vocals sound a little treated – could be mistaken – but, I feel, some studio wizardry. Keyboards are prominent with the unmistakable sound of the mellotron.

Dead Trees opens with a military drum beat. Lyrically it is very open and somewhat sad. Soaring guitar from *Dean Bennison* is worth playing this track just to hear. The bass guitar pulsates in an under-rated and melodic fashion while keyboards come to the fore as the track concludes with sound effects.

Hitchhiking to Byzantium is, of course, the title track and a glorious ten minute 'mini-epic'. The array of instruments used on this track clearly high-light the talent within *Anubis* – a track to please the aural senses. Three female voices offer 'angelic' support to great effect. It ends with some beautiful piano and is a standout from the album.

Blood is thicker than Common Sense. Sung in an almost 'rap' style with backing harmonies and great bass lines this is a track I personally rate very highly. It retains the 'cinematic feel' and equally displays all the progressive elements for which Anubis is renowned. The swirling organ adds a 'Jon Lord' touch to proceedings with bass again providing some wonderful moments before the track fades.

Tightening the Screws begins with acoustic guitar and feels like a continuation from the previous track. The use of the novachord and mellotron are interesting. *David Eaton* has said (regarding the mellotron) that he "consciously tried to limit the use of it as it had been such a staple of my sound palette". I, for one, love the sound and so glad to hear it in all its glory and used so expertly.

Partitionists, opens with piano and sound-scapes and seductively draws one into this track before it breaks out vocally. The soaring guitar returns as the track picks up pace with keyboards and bass providing the back-ground sound. Lyrically superb it ends with the sombre verse;

Your coins can't take away
They can't postpone
The cold reality
of your own headstone.

Crimson stained romance employs harmonium and church organ with some 'Floydian' harmonies, orchestration and the return of the angelic choir from '*Katrina, Becky* and *Sarah*'. This is a track which has everything the prog fan could wish for, and more. The drums are solid (as with all the tracks) but seem more to the fore here before it segues into the penultimate track.

A Room with a View is an epic track in seven sections (denoted by roman numerals). It commences with, almost inaudible, dialogue before the haunting piano intro builds, adding drums, keyboards and bass.

Dean Bennison would have made a fine blues guitarist should he have desired. His touches throughout the entire album just leave one gobsmacked.

Around the nine minute mark we are treated to 'Tony Banks (Genesis)' style piano and flute from *Martyn Cook*.

Synthesizers kick in as the track reaches a conclusion with more superb lead guitar which then segues into the final track.

Silent Wandering Ghosts quite rightly opens with spooky piano and plaintive vocals. This is a 'haunting' note on which to end the album.

It slowly builds to the half-way mark before 'beefing' up slightly but soon returning to the haunting piano and sound-scapes.

In conclusion, I find it perplexing that some reviewers in various forums decided this was a backward step. For my part this is a progression on their previous albums and stands tall in their catalogue.

Somewhere between the completion of *A Tower of Silence* and the recording of *Hitchhicking to Byzantium Nicholas Antionette* left the band and bass 'duties' were taken up by *Robert Moulding*.

It is clear I am not a musicologist – even with three years musical theory to call upon (almost entirely forgotten) –but 'I know what I like and I like what I know' and I like this album.

Musical influences abound but never become mere copyist. Such influences include; Pink Floyd, King Crimson, Yes, Genesis and Mars Volta, to name just some. "Each album tends to react to the previous" says *David Eaton* and that is clear when listening to their albums. For instance one can hear a definite Floyd influence on one album which is clearly missing on another.

Although *Anthony Stewart (bass/vocals)* had been intro-duced his official first recording debut with *Anubis* was on *The Second Hand* (2017)

The Second Hand marked the return to a fully-fledged concept album complete with 'seventies' instrumentation – organ/mellotron/synthesizers et al – and to the cinematic and symphonic style.

The band's website offers insight to the story of 'James Osbourne-Fox' (wealthy founder and CEO of 'Global Media Group') who was discovered critical and unrespon-sive by staff in a hotel room and rushed to the New York Presbyterian Hospital.

There is also extensive background information of his life and achievements in a 'faux' newspaper (London Evening Telegraph) report on the inside of the CD.

I find it difficult to select a highlight as the album – as a cohesive whole – is the only way to listen to what I consider a 'master-piece' of modern symphonic prog and the conceptual approach, however the three sections titled "*These changing Seasons*" are superb.

In hindsight, this may have been the moment when Anubis really gelled as a unit. I rank this and *A Tower of Silence* as the very best from their catalogue.

Different Stories (2018) is quite aptly named as it re-imagines tracks of previous albums in a mostly acoustic setting and was recorded and released to fund a European tour – an on-going situation for the band – as *David Eaton* explained, "We spend everything on an album to get us there (Europe), but that's really the end goal of each record now for us"

The differences between playing Australia and Europe could not be starker "you can play to 100 people in a club

– if you're lucky – and in Europe you can play Loreley". Lorelei, Germany, is home to the annual 'Night of the Prog Festival' held in its amphitheatre (which abounds in musical history) and attracts fans from around the globe where artists can find themselves playing to thousands of appreciative listeners who 'care about the way it is done'.

For Anubis Europe is "the spiritual home of the music we make".

The resulting tour saw Anubis play Loreley on 15th July 2018 in front of the largest audience (to date) they had performed for.

It also saw the release of *Lights of Change Live in Europe 2018* (2019) a two disc set of two different (in more ways than one) concerts performed during the tour.

The first disc is *Live at Loreley* where the band performed a solid set which included; *Pages of Stone – Dead Trees – Fool's Gold – These Changing Seasons III – Silent Wandering Ghosts – Disinfected and Abused.*

As one who has never had the privilege of witnessing Anubis live this superb recording 'whets the appetite'

Disc two was far removed from the Loreley experience in that it was performed in a more intimate setting in the Netherlands. What, also makes it different is that this is a performance of the album *A Tower of Silence* in its entirety.

I have previously stated my fondness for the album but to hear it (and see on youtube) only enhanced my (already huge) appreciation for *Anubis.*

Touring also provides the band time-out on their travels to partake in childish pranks, "We're just little boys on tour" says *David. Douglas Skene* is quite proficient with the German language and is often asked to interpret for other band members – an opportunity to enter into some mischievousness. "I'll leave the rest to imagination".

In late 2019 the band announced the up-coming release for their sixth studio album *Homeless* (2020) with the release of the single *Home* (2019) in the December.

Who could have foreseen the tragic events that unfolded? Just how did the band cope on an artistic level and, equally important, financially?

The complete shut-down of music venues had a devastating effect on the industry, an industry that employs thousands of people in; administration, promotion, logistics, catering, lighting and sound, road crews and the countless number of people employed by the venues themselves.

Anubis were, obviously, not immune to the 'year from hell'.

Ironically *Homeless* "was a pretty bleak, apocalyptic, view of what the world might become", "it told of fires, floods, disease and guns", "then Australia caught fire, a bat sneezed and we all spend a year indoors".

The above quotes from *David Eaton* pretty much deal with the year 2020 from an Australian perspective. Finding a moment of humour he continues, "the next album is going to be about winning the lottery if we're going to be that bloody prophetic".

Homeless is the first *Anubis* release on vinyl (prior to the CD release) and explains why the CD listing has 'side A and side B'. It also differs from their other concept albums inasmuch as it is not a complete narrative but a single persons' perspective on various aspects of our world in 2020.

Sonically captivating and lyrically thought provoking this album adds immeasurably to their body of work to date. It is an album I have pulled off the shelf more than any other in recent times. The atmospheres 'conjured up' are clear evidence of the talent within *Anubis*.

Sydney remains their home-base and several members of the band have their own home-studio – alleviating costs and limitation on time. As a band, they also have their own rehearsal space in a warehouse with copious floor space and high-ceilings. A vast array of equipment is permanently set-up. Very cost effective.

As New South Wales did not experience the extreme lock-downs imposed in other Australian states and territories the band was a little freer to meet, rehearse and discuss future directions.

David and *Dean* co-founded (and teach at) a music academy which saw its beginnings some ten years ago. This, obviously, offers an alternative source of income.

What the future holds for *Anubis* is anyone's guess. On a personal level I look forward to more and, in particular, the re-issue of *230305*.

The band has, in fact, already performed live this year – at 'The Baroque Room, Katoomba (some 90 kilometres from Sydney) where they played *Homeless* in its entirety to a sold out audience. Here's hoping for more dates as our restrictions ease and life returns to something resembling normality.

I leave the final words to *David Eaton* himself.

"What could be better than travelling across the world with your best mates, having a ball, playing the music you wrote in front of an audience that cares about it the way you do?"

CALIGULA'S HORSE

"WHAT'S IN A NAME?" This quote from Shakespeare's Romeo and Juliet (spoken by Juliet) was in reference to the unimportant nature of names. Juliet further notes, 'that a rose by any other name would smell just as sweet'.

Using this analogy for *Caligula's Horse* one could say the band by any other name would sound just as good.

Caligula's Horse it was, but why?

Sam Vallen had assembled the majority of the album *Moments from Ephemeral City* (2011) but "it was going to be titled *Caligula's Horse*". The original idea was to release the album as a solo venture under his name.

It was always considered that *Jim Grey* would sing *Alone in the World* with "other vocalists on different tracks", some of which had already been recorded.

Working together led to "finding a lot of common ground" and the tracks were re-recorded with *Jim Grey*, who also co-composed with *Vallen* the track *City has no Empathy*. *Vallen* and *Grey* are also credited with *Colossus* and *Vanishing Rites*.

Geoff Irish (drums) and *Dave Couper* (bass guitar) from *Quandary* –*Vallen's* previous band – along with *Zac Greensill* (guitar) completed the line-up. *Caligula's Horse* then became the band name for their debut album.

It is difficult to imagine the band being called anything but *Caligula's Horse* such has been their impact during the last ten years. It appears to be an inspired choice and one that resonates with prog fans from Brisbane to Buenos Aries and all points between.

April 2011 saw the release of *Moments from Ephemeral City* (2011) and the reception was enough to convince them to put a band together even if they had "no intentions beyond getting the music out there".

As a debut album, how does it sound and more important how was it received by prog fans?

The vast majority of forums and reviews I have read are not just favourable but effusively so. It would not be stretching a point to state that *Caligula's Horse* made an immediate impact.

The City has no Empathy opens the album and immediately grabs the attention of the listener however, the next track *Silence* slows things down with a beautiful acoustic feel enhanced by subtle electric guitar and keyboards and, for me, is best on the album.

Singularity picks up the tempo again and has a prog/metal feel – it is a relatively short track and one of two instrumentals.

Following is *Alone in the World* and by contrast has a duration of around eleven minutes containing some superb piano and plaintive vocals

The superb flow of the album retains one's attention right through to the amazing final track *Vanishing Rites*.

Vanishing Rites begins with a very 'jazzy' feel and 'lounge type' vocals before bursting in a totally different direction and then returning to the jazzy feel. Midway through the motif changes again. There is so much packed into those five minutes that it has never lost its appeal for me.

Brisbane is the band's home base even should *Sam Vallen* never have lived there. "I'm an hour south on the Gold Coast, and much prefer it down here". Anyone who has visited both would clearly see the attraction of the Gold Coast to Brisbane – no offence to Brisbane (it is a lovely city). It is in fact where the band records wherever they can find a facility "that seems right for the job and the budget", although Vallen does still record at home. He is also the Producer.

It was just over a year later that their second album appeared and consolidated their position. Not to mention all the touring in support of their debut.

The Tide, the Thief and River's End (2012) maintains the line-up from their debut and highlights a 'tightness' which only comes with performing together.

It is a concept album which incorporates various instruments not played by the band members and includes; flute, strings, clarinet, electric piano on *All is quiet by the Wall* performed by Sean Thomas and an assorted 'choir' of 'screamers, shouters and singers'.

Conceptually about an uprising by rebels (The Tide) the story is one of struggle to find a new home (River's End) and freedom from oppression. There is short narrative before some of the printed lyrics. I was reminded of the song 'Won't get fooled again' by the Who and, in particular, the line "meet the new boss, same as the old boss".

Whereas the prog/metal style is obvious it does not begin to do justice to *Caligula's Horse* as they are more than capable of adding touches of jazz, blues and wonderful vocal harmonies.

One track I particularly love is the short and acoustically themed *Thief* – the omnipresent character of the story.

A frenetic burst of touring to support the album saw the band undertaking an intense tour in Australia which included 'Progfest Sydney' in 2013 and 'Progfest Melbourne' 2014.

Opinion regarding audience support of prog in Australia as opposed to Europe often reveals that many bands fair better overseas but *Sam Vallen* does not see it that way feeling that "the differences are often a little overrated".

The record label 'Inside Out' was to pursue an interest in the band and sign them before the release of their next full-length studio album. 'Inside Out' has proved very influential in bringing many artists to the public's attention and 'putting money where their mouth is'. This kind of 'heavyweight' backing could only prove beneficial.

High street record stores are like 'hen's teeth' these days. Australia does boast one large retailer which still stocks a variety of music. Included is; blues, jazz, pop, alternative and heavy metal. Anything that fails to fall within the main categories (prog for instance) is filed under 'heavy metal'. Aware of this tendency I always carefully browse the 'heavy metal' shelves.

In this way I came across *Bloom* (2015) and was immediately drawn by the cover art and band name and so I purchased the album – nothing ventured, nothing gained.

This proved to be my starting point with *Caligula's Horse* and the beginning of seeking out other recordings, avidly reading the UK publication 'Prog' to avoid missing any news on forth-coming releases.

Bloom is a beautiful album with so many musical 'twists and turns' within the eight tracks that I just instinctively knew this was a band which would find its way into my collection. Discovering they are Australian only fuelled and intensified my search.

The line-up was the same as the first two albums and again the musicianship and composition are amazing. I was amused that *Sam Vallen* was credited with 'guitar and everything else'.

The captivating intro of the first and title track sets a standard which never dips. My personal favourites include; *Marigold, Firelight, Dragonfly, Turntail and Daughter of the Mountain* – that equates to more than half the album! The final track *Undergrowth* ends the album in a similar vein to the opening track.

Again, there was touring, both before and after the release, and saw them make their first appearances in Europe. In a further aside to the differences between Australia and Europe *Sam Vallen* did note "there is perhaps a greater sense of excitement in a lot of European countries – sing-a-longs and chants are a lot more acceptable"

Obviously touring brings its own highs and lows and some events that will remain indelibly stamped in the memory. One such event occurred during this 2015 tour which was related in such a way that I cannot paraphrase it and do it justice so I will quote verbatim *Sam Vallen's* response to me.

"Our first European tour of late 2015 had a handful of fairly unique experiences attached to it. We played Paris a few days after the horrific shooting at the Bataclan, when the place was still under a State of Emergency. When the attacks happened we were in Germany, and we had to deeply consider whether the show would (or indeed, could) go ahead. We decided that we'd try, with the caveat that those feeling unsafe in any way should not attend, a message we pushed on our social media and so forth. We thought it was an important gesture to attempt to play the show, whether it was able to happen or not. We got into Paris fine and it was unlike any of us imagined; starkly empty streets (almost) bereft of tourists. We played a truly loving show which felt like it was to a home crowd. On the merch stand that night we heard from multiple people about friends who had been wounded and killed a handful of nights prior, and how much our presence in the city meant to them. It was a reminder of the fact that, as humble and insignificant our platform is in a larger sense, it means something to many people. It might have been couched in tragedy, but it ended up being a beautiful night that none of us will forget"

Paris is my and Louise's favourite destination when we visit Europe and we never miss the opportunity to spend a few days there. We have visited during every season of the year and always found it vibrant and overflowing with tourists – regardless of the weather. To read how the band found the city brought a lump to my throat and a feeling of empathy for the people caught up in those horrific events. For their collective response to the tragedy and willingness to travel and play Paris under such conditions all I can say is 'hats off'!

Back in Australia the band experienced the first line-up change mid-2016 when *Geoff Irish* left to be replaced by *Josh Griffin*. This was followed in early 2017 when *Zac Greensill* decided to concentrate on a side project (*Opus of a Machine*) and was replaced by *Adrian Goleby*.

It was this line-up who appeared on their next album which also proved be the last to include *Dave Couper*.

In Contact (2017) was another conceptual album with five main themes and, in my opinion, the most 'prog' sounding in their catalogue complete with 'proggy' cover art.

To the Wind is a four part 'suite' consisting of; *Dream of the Dead/ Will's Song (let the colours run)/The hands are the hardest/Love conquers all,* and bursts from the speakers with some stellar guitar, pounding drums and typical vocals from *Jim Grey* – a superbly underrated vocalist and compliment to the music. Around the five minute mark it all changes with some lighter ambient sounds prior the pulsating bass and Gilmouresque guitar. It is an absolutely wonderful opening track. *Dave Couper's* bass seems to me more prominent than previously. Part three '*Hands*' is lush and almost totally acoustic with incredible harmonies.

The Caretaker (Songs for no one/Capulet) opens with busy vocal and guitar and a steady beat. The pace continues throughout with a few slower moments here and there. *Capulet* begins acoustically and the vocal is almost 'Celtic' in feel particularly when the harmonising 'choir' join in gloriously.

Ink (Fill my heart/Inertia and the weapon of the wall/The Cannon's Mouth) is another multiple part offering which begins slowly and grows. The protagonist rants and raves – at times not totally coherent – just as well there are printed lyrics. Part three captures more of the prog/metal element albeit with a toned-down feel and some more superb lead guitar.

Graves concludes the album in fine form. Again it is a multi-part consisting of; *Faint Heart/A few peaceful years/The boy and the broken wheel/Hands shape stone.* At around 15 minutes it is lengthy but never loses its appeal – bordering between metal and rock with guitar lines, at times reaching ethereal moments, it is the 'masterpiece' from the album.

This was an album fully embraced by the progressive and metal communities and garnered critical acclaim.

Dave Couper's departure in 2018 was, mainly, to do with health reasons, however financial and other considerations also loomed large. His replacement proved to be *Dale Prinsse*. He was well known to all for his mixing and production work as well as playing alongside *Zac Greensill* in *Opus of a Machine*.

This line-up; *Jim Grey* – lead vocals, *Dave Prinsse* – bass, *Adrian Goleby* – guitar, *Josh Griffin* – drums and *Sam Vallen* – lead guitar (and everything else) set out in late 2019 on the bands' first tour to America (including South America).

"Latin America is actually probably the place that surprised us the most" says *Sam Vallen*. With regard to audience response he continues, "...they don't just sing along to lyrics, they sing along to guitar solos and melodies, which is obviously wonderful for me!"

As the year closed *Caligula's Horse* were plotting their next album which would be followed by more touring and then...

2020 proved itself a year in which the entire globe suffered when a mutant strain of the flu (Covid-19) decimated livelihoods, economies, businesses and wrought a frightening number of fatalities as well as untold mental and psychological problems.

The music industry (live performance in particular) would enter an unwanted hiatus. *Caligula's Horse* toured at a prolific pace so the pandemic "decimated our regular income streams". It also "compromised the band". *Sam Vallen* does say that the band is fortunate in that "albums and merch sell, but the income is secondary to the sense of "being" – meeting our fans and performing around the world". He did, however, see this current line-up remaining together and "waiting to get back into recording and touring".

As we all endured lockdown(s) and restrictions musicians around the world found themselves with unprecedented time on their hands as evidenced by the amount of albums released – including one from *Caligula's Horse*, right in the middle of a severe five month lockdown here in Victoria.

Rise Radiant (2020) appeared in May and was eagerly anticipated by fans. My copy was obtained on-line as (almost) all businesses were forced to close.

The cover art again grabbed my attention – a large buck complete with majestic antlers and facing a snow-capped mountain – it is brilliant and reflects the album's title wonderfully.

My immediate response was (Amazon review) as follows;

"Having played this album three times I have to admit my first listen was anything but favourable. I own all previous releases by CH and was quite excited about this release.

My first impressions were quite negative. Undeterred I played it again and thought perhaps I was being too critical as it struck me as a slow burner. On a third listen it finally got me, man this is good stuff.

It has to be said that here is one great Aussie gem totally unappreciated in their own backyard. The release date came and went with no mention by so-called music gurus on TV and nothing in newspaper entertainment sections. Powderfingers' lockdown concert gathered all the plaudits.

I find it quite annoying that these guys are more of a draw in Europe than at home. I know the words progressive and metal in the same sentence is as appealing to some as watching grass grow but to describe them thus is a disservice and very misleading.

The surprise here is in the bonus tracks; *Peter Gabriel's* "Don't give up" and *Split Enz* "Message to my Girl".

Surprisingly, the first is amazingly good and almost vies as best track except that *SALT* is so glorious and the vocal harmonies fantastic.

Other standout tracks, in my opinion, are the opener *The Tempest* and *Valkyrie*. The track that took me most by surprise is *Resonate* which I have to say is unlike anything else I've heard from the band.

All-in-all it is worth investing a little time with this one as it doesn't immediately hit the spot like their other albums but is truly up there as "close to best".

When I suggested to *Sam Vallen* that it was not as accessible as their previous albums his response appeared as though he had taken offence, "accessibility is a very subjective thing" – I hope he didn't as no offense was intended and I did go on to say it was ultimately more satisfying.

Rise Radiant is intended to present songs which stand on their own as opposed to the flow of conceptual albums such as *In Contact* and achieved its aim admirably. It is intended to "feel more like Nevermind (Nirvana) or the Black Album (AC/DC)".

The time that has passed has only strengthened my view that *Rise Radiant* is a superb album and it receives high rotation from me.

At the time of writing almost a year has passed and Victoria again finds itself in lockdown with the so-called 'Indian Strain' having been imported into the state. This means that everything is back on hold and that includes live performance.

I have yet to see the band perform live and thought that, as things seemed to be improving, venues would re-open and live music would make a welcome return. Not to be – yet!

It only remains for me to thank *Sam Vallen* for generously giving his time to answer my questions in a thoughtful way and look forward to the band 'rising radiantly' once restrictions are passed and life returns to some semblance of normality.

THE CHURCH

THE CHURCH, WHO HAVE been in existence in one form or another for the last forty years, have released some twenty-six albums as well as numerous singles, compilations and videos, are still, to this day, remembered for the hugely successful single *Under the Milky Way* (1988).

The single was taken from the equally successful album *Starfish* (1988) and was, at one stage, not even considered for inclusion on the album. It was almost an after-thought as most of the band (reportedly) hated it. Even *Steve Kilbey* had doubts about the track but was swayed when record executives deemed it a sure-fire hit single – wrong more often than right, they certainly 'hit the nail on the head' with their choice. The rest, as they say, is history. It still receives airplay on 'classic rock' stations such as Gold FM here in Melbourne.

That was some eight years after their formation and things had settled – as much as any period in their history could be considered settled – and they were all giving 100 per cent.

To categorise *The Church* is quite difficult. *Kilbey* likes to think of the band as 'Aussie Hippies' and basically psyche-delic. That they also displayed traits of some of their heroes (notably David Bowie) as well as crafting some beautiful ambient sounds and arguably venturing into progres-sive, they remain unlike any other band one chooses to name.

Formed in Canberra, Australia in 1980 the band was the brainchild of lyricists and songwriter *Steven (Steve) Kilbey* who played bass and keyboards as well as being the vocalist.

The first incarnation of the band also included; *Peter Koppes* (guitar, vocals, keyboards), *Marty Willson-Piper* (guitars and vocals) and *Nick Ward* (drums). Drummers were a (it would unfold) problem within the band and *The Church* would see that position change more than any other.

In order to establish *the Church,* a torturous round of never ending gigs was undertaken but the band had difficulty gaining acceptance of their music amid the post-punk genre and the emergence of the so-called 'shoe gazers' and new wave and romantic music which was gaining momentum to (almost) the exclusion of everything else.

Of Skins and Heart (1981) proved to be the first full-length studio album, providing the hit single *The Unguarded Moment* – which would establish the band.

As a debut *Of Skins and Heart* is a good beginning, if a little uneven, and displays some trade-mark '*Church*' sound which was, at this stage, only hinted at.

The Unguarded Moment is clearly the best track on the album and an obvious choice for single release. The guitar interplay and bass lines along with *Kilbey's* vocals are an early indication of the evolving style present on subsequent albums.

Most of the album has a very early eighties feel, which may seem a churlish thing to say but *The Church* did go on to produce a sound which was 'out-of-step' with the bulk of bands they competed with.

The true indicator of what was to come presents itself with *Is this where you live.* It creates atmosphere and highlights superb guitar work from Koppes – a little Enoesque. *Nick Ward's* drumming reveals great technique but he was to be replaced before the next album.

Nick Ward was truly *Steve Kilbey's* nemesis and failed to endear himself to the rest of the band. He appeared to be the proverbial 'square peg' who took great delight in upsetting as many people as possible. It was no surprise to insiders and some observers that his tenure was short-lived.

His replacement proved himself very capable behind the kit. Surprising, though, was the fact he was several years younger than the other three members of the band. His youthful exuberance clearly shines through and rubbed off on the others.

Richard Ploog (Ploogy) was born in 1962 so is therefore 8 years *Kibley's* junior. He appeared to have 'energy to burn' and played in other bands at the same time – notably 'Beasts of Bourbon'.

The Blurred Crusade (1982) released less than a year after their debut is a marked improvement and the developing style is in evidence.

There is less 'in your face' rock and most tracks are slower with better lyrics. This – as with their debut – was produced by *Bob Clearmountain*, who clearly was able to get the best from each musician.

Fields of Mars, in my opinion, is the real stand-out track from the album however, the track chosen as a single was *Almost with You* – which emulated *The Unguarded Moment* in chart position but not overall popularity.

An Interlude and *Secret Corners* are both glorious tracks with the former offering some stunning guitar while *You Took*, in all its eight-minute glory, borders on 'prog' and 'Bowie' simultaneously. The guitar is a little buried in the mix for my liking. It sounds amazingly good despite that.

The Church has been likened to; Pretenders, U2, the Beatles, Pink Floyd, the Moody Blues and David Bowie. Clearly it is difficult to sound like all of them and my personal feeling is that some struggled to define their sound and clutched at straws over snippets of music which may have sounded like someone else. *The Church* was and remained unique throughout most of their (on-going) career.

Whatever transpired between the making of *'Blurred'* and *Seance* (1983) is pure speculation but as a unit they sounded anything but unified. Certainly a quantity of substances seemed readily available at the time and some relationships – band and otherwise – appeared strained. The resulting album was far from a classic. A review I read described it as a masterpiece of 'dreamy psychedelic pop' and compared them to; the Cure, the Smiths and Echo and the Bunnymen, among others, before stating they "sound like no-one else". I feel vindicated with my 'clutching at straws' theory.

This release proved to be one of a number of times when *the Church* 'shot themselves in the foot' and 'pulled defeat from the jaws of victory'.

Three albums in just over two years followed by a gap of over two years before the next, left some feeling they had 'had-their-day'. Nothing could be further from the truth.

Hey Day (1985) not only proved the doubters wrong but also was the first to fully incorporate the signature sound that continues to this day.

The front cover has a picture of the band looking the part of the hippy band (note those dreadful paisley shirts) they conceived themselves to be and immediately dates the album.

Myrrh opens the album and is unforgettable in its lush-ness and delivery – a track which I revisit often.

Already Yesterday, Columbus, Tantalized and *Disenchanted* all had release as singles at some stage, with varying degrees of success. None proved a 'hit'.

For my part, the real highlight from the album is *Happy Hunting Ground*. It has a psychedelic/prog feel with a drum pattern similar to a military beat. Purely instrumental this wonderful track is a foretaste of things to come.

Steven Kilbey's vocal performances show maturity and that oft noted 'talk/sing' style.

In all I consider this to be the best album to date but another two year break had the effect of some disconnect within the band which would require a remarkable follow-up album to 'mend fences' and bring the fan-base back on board.

In all fairness the band was touring at a frenetic pace but with mixed reactions and – at times – a less than a totally enthusiastic performance. Equally some press conferences and label required obligations were met with unfavourable indifference by the band as a whole and *Steve Kilbey* in particular.

Starfish (1988) was and remains a remarkable album and proved *The Church* had an arsenal of sounds and ideas to match anyone. The *Kilbey* penned poem which adorns the original vinyl added to the mystique of both its author and the band.

Remembered and revered primarily for the single *Under the Milky Way* this was a break-through that awakened the listening public to the potential of the band. It was the first time many had heard the band and even today when I am in conversation and mention the *Church* I still get a reactionary frown which indicates their unfamiliarity with the name. *Under the Milky Way* will then be song (sort of in tune) and the reaction immediately changes. Oh yeah I know the *Church* – clearly they don't.

This is an album which is still played from start to finish and refuses to age, be pigeon-holed or lose its appeal.

I had only arrived in Australia the previous October but was familiar with the band and bought the album when it was released. Suddenly 'every man and his dog' would be singing the praises of the album and, in particular, the single. I only met one guy who 'knew' the band and brought to my home all their previous releases but did tellingly say that "some did not even realise they are Australian".

Now, as never before, was the time to capitalise.

It was almost exactly two years before their next album was released.

Gold Afternoon Fix (1990) proved to be an album brimming with good ideas but 'treading water' to some extent. It has the feel of going through the motions. Perhaps the recording of the solo album by *Kilbey Remindlessness* (1990) and the side project album by *Jack Frost* (1990) was a case too many irons in the fire. His 'well publicised' heroin intake began around this time too and extended for some considerable time – at great cost on many fronts – and could not have been advantageous. His battle with the 'white lady' was, eventually, won – with more than a little help from 'Krishna'.

Many have cited it as a disappointment after the amazing *Starfish*. While it does not achieve the heights of its predecessor it is (overall) a pleasing album – albeit one that does not leave the shelf too often.

Tracks that standout are; *Pharaoh, Terra Nova Cain, Russian Autumn Heart, You're still Beautiful, Grind* and *Laughing.*

Laughing starts with superb ambience and understated guitar before the unmistakable vocals of *Steve Kilbey*. The title seems ironic given that there seemed little (lyrically) to laugh about!

Grind is in fact the final track and closes wonderfully a 'less than' wonderful album, however I do feel that much of the criticism it received was unwarranted.

The rest of the 'nineties' proved prolific with, arguably, some of their best material surfacing during the decade. Equally, *Steven Kilbey* was busy with solo material and numerous projects.

Priest=aura (1992) proved another massive (second) break-through album. It seems churlish to call it a 'break-through' when the band had been going well over twelve years at this stage but the highs and lows in their catalogue could be stark on occasions and certainly frustrating for fans.

Jay Dee Daugherty now occupied the drum-stool but that was not the final change. *Daugherty* played with; Patti Smith, Mark Knopfler, Joey Ramone, Billy Idol and many others in a colourful career before joining the *Church* and staying some three years.

Personally, I love this album as I feel it edges so close to 'prog' and warrants inclusion within the genre.

From the opening track *aura* to the instrumental closing track *film* there is not a weak moment, in fact there are even some moments of humour, not least the short and quirky *witch hunt*.

Other standouts include; *paradox, the disillusionist* and *chaos* with the latter being the longest and best of album, in my opinion.

Sometime Anywhere (1994), *Magician among the Spirits* (1996) and *Hologram of Baal* (1998) marked a period I find matchless in their career and any of these albums are more than worthy inclusions to their catalogue.

Hologram of Baal was issued as a limited edition two disc set for the first pressings.

The second disc, titled *Bastard Universe* was a continuous piece broken into six parts and totally instrumental. Psychedelic in nature and coming in at almost eighty minutes it may have proved hard for some to assimilate. I found it wonderful and play it when at home alone with the lights down and no distractions. It can take the listener out of their comfort zone.

Meanwhile *Daugherty* had departed and eventually replaced by *Tim Powles* in 1996. *Peter Koppes* also left but soon returned.

A very interesting album was to appear during this period from a band going by the name *The Refo:mation*.

Pharmakoi/distance crunching honchos with echo units (1997) is an unwieldy title. Anyone coming across the album and reading the band members names would find, *Kilbey, Koppes* and *Powles* listed along with two guests.

It may seem reasonable to assume that this 'side project' would present something completely different from *the Church*. Initially, perhaps that may be so, but it soon becomes apparent that this is *the Church* in all but name.

The opening track is *1:07* and an ambient introduction lasting one minute and seven seconds! From there on it proved difficult to differentiate this album from, say, *Magicians among the Spirits* which was released a year before.

After twenty years *Steve Kilbey* carried his band through to the new millennium still displaying a work ethic that beggars belief. To list the various side projects, appearances and solo work would be exhaustive and impossible in a book designed purely as 'an introduction'. It is difficult enough to include every Church album released so you, dear reader, may need to do some serious research.

Forget Yourself (2003) proved the next album to gain my attention – not that those released prior are bad albums.

At this stage the line-up was; *Steve Kilbey, Peter Koppes, Tim Powles* and *Marty Willson-Piper*. The only photo appears on the back cover showing four men looking a little 'world-weary' and appears to be the balcony of a pub or hotel. It belies the musical content which is anything but weary. An album beautifully crafted and executed – an example of *the Church* at their very best. It is psychedelic in places but with trade-mark ambience and (naturally) the unmistakeable vocals of *Kilbey*.

It proved the bench-mark for the releases during the remainder of the decade and beyond.

Two albums released in 2004 (a matter of two months apart) are worth consideration.

El Momento Descuidado (2004) revisits some of their catalogue while offering five new songs – *0408/November/ All I know/'till the cows come home/Between Mirages* (the latter being instrumental). The title is actually a rough Spanish rendering of *The Unguarded Moment*.

The album was recorded acoustically and a short acoustic tour followed.

The title track is a major re-invention while *Under the Milky Way* is truer to the original. The whole 'sound' of the album is a departure from the ambience and layered textures of the past, a bit 'warts-and-all' but beautifully done.

Beside Yourself (2004) was released prior to *El Momento Descuidado* and is a collection of out-takes from the *Forget Yourself* sessions. It received a limited edition release in Australia only and consequently acquiring a copy may prove financially out of reach for some. Should you discover one for less than US$50 snap it up. It is a great addition to the parent album. In the U.S. the original album was released with a bonus disc which includes some of these tracks but again the cost may prove inhibitive.

The remainder of the decade would see a further five releases including *El Momento Siquiente* (2007) and is similar to *El Momento Descuidado* with all tracks being acoustic. Three new tracks appear among the fourteen on offer, once again, it concludes with an instrumental.

Untitled #23 (2009) was universally praised as the best album in their catalogue. It saw release through the bands' own label in Australia and by 'Second Motion Records' in America. It derived its title simply for being their 23rd full album release.

In my opinion *Untitled #23* is the last great album from the *Kilbey, Koppes, Powles* and *Willson-Piper* line-up. It retains the atmospheres, musicianship, vocals and song-writing long associated with the band. It also remains a firm favourite of the author.

Second Motion Records proved a 'thorn in the side' of *Steve Kilbey*. He considered the treatment of '*The Church*' by the label nothing short of "insulting" and even tendered his resignation from the band while urging people not to purchase anything released by the label. Although their albums sold well the band saw precious little reward.

By late 2013 the band re-grouped without *Marty Willson-Piper*. His replacement was *Ian Haug* from *Powderfinger,* who joined the band for the recording of their next album. The parting of ways may not have been harmonious but suffice to say there are two sides to every story. It may have caused mixed feelings for fans with many lamenting the absence of *Willson-Piper*.

Over five years passed before a new release but what a memorable album awaited fans.

Further/Deeper (2014) was issued through *unorthodox* (the band label) and MGM.

It represents a band maturing but still offering up large doses of ambience mixed with superb guitar work (both lead and bass) and drumming which mines a variety of styles but is always complimentary to the other instruments. It is the vocals which, naturally, add that *Church* feel we all know and love. *Further/Deeper* is a brilliant album on every conceivable level.

A band celebrating its 35th year with a body of work almost on a par with *Van Morrison's* output without displaying his single-mindedness. This is impressive enough but running parallel are the solo albums and various projects which translates to hundreds of songs composed – fully or in part – by *Steve Kilbey*.

Released earlier the same year was the amazing *A Psychedelic Symphony: Live at Sydney Opera House*. Should you have not realised that *The Church* were back and firing on all cylinders you may have missed this album and now it is almost impossible to track down. The album is a showcase for the album *Further/Deeper* which is performed in its entirety.

During 2014/15 the band toured Australia and America presenting the album on a regular basis with new member *Ian Haug* receiving plaudits from *Kilbey*.

Check out their concert from Barcelona on youtube.

Man Woman Life Death Infinity (2017) "This is The Church's water album" according to *Steve Kilbey*. It is certainly an album that 'flows' nicely and the water element is very apparent. Many reviewers awarded it a five star rating, singing its praises and commenting on the 'veteran' bands validity on their 25th studio release. I whole-heartedly agree.

2020 brought many things into focus and *The Church* should have been celebrating their 40th anniversary in style. The news early in the year that *Peter Koppes* had decided to leave facilitated touring member *Jeffrey Cain* becoming a full member of the band. The news for the remainder of the year and into 2021 was full of doom and gloom as the pandemic caused havoc around the world. At the time of writing we are still under restrictions and partial lock-downs.

The official website also announced a new album was being worked on with the 'working title' *In the wake of the Zeitgeist*. As of mid-2021 nothing has materialised and the last entry on the website is the cancellation of their aptly named *Cruel World Tour*.

Let's hope this situation changes soon and *The Church* emerge with more to offer as I, for one, feel they still have a lot of fuel left in their tank.

DEAD
LETTER
CIRCUS

OCHRE WAS AN AUSTRALIAN progressive metal band active from 1996 until 2003. They issued two eps: *Awakenings* (2001) and *Horizon* (2002) – both are difficult to track down.

The nucleus of the band, namely *Kim Benzie* (vocals and keyboards) and *Stewart Hill* (bass), went on to form *Dead Letter Circus* along with *Rob Maric* (guitar) and *Scott Davey* (drums and percussion) in Brisbane around 2004.

Dead Letter Circus have since been described as 'alternative rock' and likened to *Radiohead, Soundgarden* and *Karnivool*, just to name a few – not bad company!

Releasing a self-titled ep and some singles the band soon came to the attention of the Australian Broadcasting Corporation's youth station triple j through the single *Disconnect and Apply* (2007) – which received heavy rotation.

Dead Letter Circus's profile was raised considerably enabling them to perform at festivals across Australia, most notably 'Big Day Out' in Melbourne, 'Come Together' in Sydney and 'Over-Cranked' in Brisbane, playing alongside the likes of: *Judas Priest, Karnivool* and *The Butterfly Effect.* They also toured extensively as the headline act across Australia.

Original drummer *Scott Davey* departed in late 2008. His replacement was *Luke Williams* previously playing (mainly) with *Melodyssey* who performed in similar style to *Dead Letter Circus.*

This is the Warning (2010) was released on 14th May 2010 – which just happens to be the birthday of 'yours truly' – thanks guys. It made an immediate impact debuting at number 1 on the ARIA Album Chart. A tour in support the album saw them playing in most Australian capital cities and raised their profile ever higher. Headlining another Australian tour in 2011 their support act was *Floating Me* (often stylised as *FloatingMe*) – more on them in the next chapter.

It came as no surprise that the album was well performed, recorded and produced, given that the band members had done the 'hard yards' for many years.

The album itself saw the inclusion of some earlier single releases and is true to the 'alternative' descriptor while also displaying elements of 'prog' and 'prog/metal'. It contains a couple of real stand out tracks which are, in my opinion, *Drum* and the title track which close the album. *Drum* (no surprise here) highlights the playing of *Luke Williams* who is a superb and energetic drummer. *This is the Warning,* commences with radio signal beeps and a 'disconnected' voice before the vocals kick in. Lyrically it can be taken a couple of ways but, for my part, I see this as 'a warning' regarding the postulations of those who would have us all toeing the 'party-line'. Considering our political situation at present in our 'over-governed' states our politicians would do well to heed the message here.

The majority of 2011 saw *Dead Letter Circus* touring the United Kingdom, U.S.A., where they played support to *Animals as Leaders,* before returning to Australia. Another tour followed under the title 'No Fracking Way'. 'Fracking' is the process to extract oil or gas from subterranean rocks by injecting liquid at high pressure to force open existing fissures. In Australia's case it was coal seam gas and *Rob Maric* wanted to raise public awareness of the inherent dangers of the practise.

In 2012 work started on a new album. The album was conceived as a lyrical follow-up to the issues explored in their debut album. It was mid 2013 before the release materialised.

2013 also witnessed the departure of founding member *Rob Maric* to be replaced with another ex-Melodyssey member *Clint Vincent.*

By the time the album was released the line-up had grown to six – *Kim Benzie* vocals, *Stewart Hill* bass, *Tom Skerlj* guitar, *Luke Palmer* guitar, *Clint Vincent* guitar and *Luke Williams* drums.

The Catalyst Fire (2013) is indeed an album brimming with thought provoking lyrics while the musical ideas are furthered. At times it has a prog/metal assault but not assaulting the aural senses. It is incredibly difficult to pull out one track as a highlight as the whole album is an experience to be savoured, however on a personal level the opening track is amazing with a sound not unlike ship fog horns blasting. *Lost without Leaders* is equally impressive with lyrics to match and closing track *Kachina* – A Kachina is an ancestral spirit of the Peublo Indians and the lyrics appear to make reference to prophecies – is superb and makes one want to play the whole thing again.

Later in the year the band performed a number of 'sold out' acoustic shows which contained re-imagined songs from the album. Then an acoustic 'mini-album' featuring six songs – my copy has eight songs, two of which are taken from live performance at the 'Toff' – titled *Stand Apart* (2013). The second live track *One Step* is from the album *'This is the Warning'.* Superb musicianship is on display and in all honestly it was impossible to tell when the first 'live' track kicked in with only the audience applause confirming it was 'live'. *Dead Letter Circus* would revisit this idea again to great effect and I really enjoyed this departure – there have been some less than appreciative comments on various forums, which I find totally perplexing.

During 2014 *Dead Letter Circus* started work on their third full-length album which saw release the following year. Fans were teased through the bands 'Twitter' posts before they finally revealed the new album would be called *Aesthesis*.

Aesthesis (2015) was released in the August and went straight into the ARIA (Australian Recording Industry Association) Chart at number two, where it peaked.

The album has the same line-up as previously except for *Tom Skerlj* who departed in 2014.

The definition of aesthesis is 'an unelaborated elementary awareness of stimulation'.

The front cover depicts a human heart while the back cover has the same heart with a cortex running up to a human brain. When the disc is removed the – reassuring – words 'YOU ARE NOT ALONE' appear in large type. Certainly the lyrics depict deep emotions and experiences that are unique to humans – as far as we know. Studies do appear to indicate that certain other animals display emotion and attachment.

I have seen *Dead Letter Circus* described as 'heavy metal' but, as I have stated previously, they have a much wider palette. Whereas descriptors are important for the record buying public they can be misleading and deter some. The need to pigeon-hole a sound has been part of the record industry agenda from very early times.

Certainly with *Aesthesis* one can hear and appreciate the wider palette and in particular with the track *Silence*, which includes a performance by the *Trinity Lutheran Choir Ensemble* and enhances an already glorious song.

It is slower with intense vocal and ambience. The drums are 'busy' but not distracting while the bass stands out in places. This is my personal highlight from the album.

In 2017 *Dead Letter Circus* issued another acoustically re-imagined album containing all the tracks from their self-titled ep released in 2007. *One Step* (which was recorded live for the *Stand Apart* acoustic mini-album) received a studio recording along with four other previously recorded tracks.

These acoustic re-imaginings are just glorious in their execution. Complementing the unchanged line-up on piano and organ is *Ian Peres* with strings performed by *Chris Carmichael*.

There really is no standout track as the album as a whole flows superbly. That having been said, *Silence* is one I skip to more often than any other, with a touch of strings adding a certain ethereal quality.

The following year (2018) saw the release of *Dead Letter Circus* with the same line-up, which offered stability with the added bonus of playing together regularly and getting to know one another's strengths.

Nominated for an ARIA award in the category of 'Best Hard Rock or Heavy Metal Album' the band was pipped by *Northlane* with their album *Alien* – a truly 'metalcore' band.

Although *Dead Letter Circus* delivered a heavier album than previous releases I personally don't hear this as heavy metal, but it does border on hard rock.

The disc comes in a jewel case with an outer slip-case which offers two covers by simply removing the slip-case – which one has to in order to play it!

An Australian tour in support of the album was announced, kicking off in late November and ending just prior to Christmas. It saw the band hot foot from Western Australia through Queensland, New South Wales, Australian Capital Territory, Victoria and South Australia.

Sadly that was the last posting on their website and no further activity or information is apparent. With 2020 and 2021 seeming like total write-off's for touring bands I sincerely hope they are simply riding out the storm and come back stronger than ever.

KARNIVOOL

AUSTRALIA'S *KARNIVOOL* HAVE BEEN active since 1997. They existed prior to that, as a bunch of high school buddies in Perth, Western Australia. They were basically a covers band, playing songs by *Nirvana* and *Carcass*.

Perceived wisdom suggests that lead vocalist *Ian Kenny* set about sacking his buddies and building a new band with original songs. He also named the band from, I am reliably informed, the description associated with the previous band 'bunch of clowns' – hence *Karnivool*.

The first line-up was: *Ian Kenny, Andrew Goddard* – guitar, *Andrew Brown* – bass and *Brett McKenzie* – drums.

Perceived wisdom also suggests that *Persona* (2001) was their first release however a self-titled ep was released in 1999 and subsequently sank without trace. *Persona* included one track from their debut which was '*Some more of the same*'.

There are many reviews and opinions regarding *Persona* with the general feeling being 'it is only for the completist'. Yes, it is not to the standard of their – to date – three full-length studio albums. What it all adds up to is the highlighting of a band 'feeling' out their strengths.

The recording itself sees the inclusion of *Jon Stockman* who replaced *Andrew Brown* and *Ray Hawking* the replacement for *Brett McKenzie*.

The opening track *Fade* is fast and furious and reminiscent of *Nirvana*. However the following two tracks *Da-reka* and *Headcase* do point the way to what followed and bear the early hall-marks associated with *Karnivool*.

Featherweight opens with some very 'Floydian' guitar effects before the heavy onslaught of guitar and drums. Vocals are little 'in-your-face' but not to its detriment, with the exception of the guttural yell. Fairly lengthy at over eight minutes, it could have been edited slightly, in my opinion.

The final track is the one previously recorded for their (forgotten) debut ep '*Some more of the same*'. This segues from *Featherweight* with similar 'Floydian' effects. The bass is thunderous but a little buried in the mix with the drums prominent. Some understated guitar is quite glorious. This too, clocks in at over nine minutes but in this case would suffer with any editing.

Not just for completists and with a total duration of approximately thirty-three minutes should be considered a mini-album.

The touring circuit beckoned and although some disappointments ensued there was enough support to keep the band afloat with serious work commencing for their debut album.

Although this album is credited to the entire band (with writing and performing) it is firmly believed that *Andrew Goddard* had written and recorded the vast majority of what was to appear on their debut. What was presented to the band was 'as-good-as' the finished product. *Ray Hawkins* played drums on one track, *Lifelike*, with *Goddard* performing drums on all the others.

Themata (2005) was released independently but its impact was immense as any visit to 'prog' forums attests. The endless listener reviews extol this album as a masterpiece of modern prog/metal. Prog and rock magazines constantly make reference to the album's importance to the genre and the band itself.

High praise indeed but is it justified?

The success of *Themata* in lifting the profile of *Karnivool* cannot and, indeed, should not be underestimated and hopefully the following short analysis will convince any doubters of its importance to the band and the genre in general.

The album cover has become iconic depicting a house-fly with the two noughts in *Karnivool* replacing the insect's eyes.

My purchase of the album was after spending a pleasant afternoon browsing the shelves of a local record store renowned for the eclectic approach by the owner who carefully displayed so many genres and sub-genres that it drew in an equally eclectic mix of customers. Sadly, due to the popularity of down-loading and early retirement beckoning, he was forced to close shop but continues to offer a service on-line. Thank you Glenn – you know who you are.

Themata opens atmospherically before launching into a prog/metal attack with a couple of short acoustic breaks. The well-chosen opening track *Cote* has the desired effect of engaging the listener.

The title track is next and, in my opinion, one of the best on the album. The heavy guitars are relentless and pounding as are the drums with *Goddard* displaying proficiency on his 'non-preferred' instrument.

Shutterspeed follows with a similar intensity with *Ian Kenny's* vocals high in the mix and rightly so.

Fear of the sky is the first time I personally became aware of the bass playing and it is amazingly good. The track slows a little and becomes atmospheric around the three minute mark but not for long.

Roquefort – song about cheese! Of course not, that just happened to be the working title – apparently originally it was intended to include horns which gave it a 'cheesy feel' but the title stuck.

Some consider it to be a reference to sex however it is very ambiguous and could also be considered a song about futility. "Chasing rabbits down a hole" is hardly a fulfilling pastime. Also it could reference the futility of finding 'love' with real meaning or a fulfilling relationship. Listener discretion is advised.

Lifelike is the track with *Ray Hawkins* on drums. This is a full-on prog/metal track, highlighting his drumming against the onslaught of guitars and vocal.

Scarabs – the scarab (beetle) was revered in ancient Egypt as it represented the cycle of life, among other things. This short instrumental track is high in tension and sonically piercing. I can't say with any certainty that it is representative of the life cycle of the scarab but I'm happy to accept that interpretation.

Sewn and Silent slows things down considerably with some nice acoustic guitar and plaintive vocal.

Mauseum is not a word I was familiar with and, as it happens, nor is Google. Lyrically there is no indication as to why the track was thus titled so it is anyone's guess. I like this track with its drive and vigour again displaying a prog/metal sensibility.

Synops or SynOps has been defined as an 'assembly of talent, capabilities and technologies'. It is befitting a band which incorporates all three. On this track there is an underlying back-beat with pulsating guitar and high octave vocals.

Omitted for clarity was simply 'omitted for clarity' and contains just a few seconds of silence. Happily it leads into *Change (Part I)* which is atmospheric and a total departure from everything that's gone before. The vocals sound not unlike *Peter Gabriel* during his *Genesis* period. It is a track which gives the impression it is building up to something before suddenly ending.

Themata is a debut album to rival any and the instrumental virtuosity and lyricism deliver in such a way as to attract all the plaudits mentioned earlier. Listening to the album, while penning my thoughts, it is not hard to understand its reception and acceptance.

During early 2007 the band signed to an Indie label in America and the album was issued in both the US and the UK along with the re-release of *Persona* later in that year. As a result they toured North America playing 'The Great American Rampage Tour'. By the time 2008 rolled in they found themselves back in Australia and in the studio to work on the follow up to *Themata*.

The follow-up proved to be more of a band effort than their debut.

Before any release more touring, in particular touring of Australia, which saw the band perform at many of Australia's large festivals – Big Day Out, Pyramid Rock, Southbound and Homebake – playing material slated for the new album.

Sound Awake (2009) had the line-up of: *Ian Kenny* (vocals), *Drew Goddard* (guitar), *Mark Hosking* (guitar), *Jon Stockman* (bass) and *Steve Judd* (drums). *Steve Judd* played on all tracks except *Set fire to the Hive* which featured *Dave Parkin*.

On its release it debuted at #2 in the ARIA album charts. It was also certified 'Gold' in Australia for sales – although sales certification required fewer sales in comparison to America or England – it was, nonetheless, an amazing result.

The album itself was to display a slightly 'toned down' sonic assault and proved somewhat more eclectic in approach. Some tracks showing a band maturity without relying on volume alone.

If pressed to select one track for the uninitiated it would be *New Day.* For my part this sums up the great leaps the band had made and is extremely representative of the album in general. This is one brilliant album from an evolving band. It may seem like heresy to some but I have a preference for *Sound Awake* over *Themata.* As good as the latter was this album rates higher with me most probably because it is more prog leaning and less metal.

On the back of the initial success of the album more touring was required to support and promote it further and again Australia was hit hard followed by New Zealand. A real 'feather-in-the-cap' was their headlining 'Third Eye Gathering' in Los Angeles. From there it was unto the UK and Europe before returning to the US. Then back to Australia where shows soon became 'sold out' and further shows needed to be added. All this hectic globe-trotting activity enhanced their reputation and profile.

The most astounding concert proved to be to a reported 10,000 audience in Mumbai, India. The band did not realise they had a following in India with *Goddard* commenting after the concert, "What the hell? Did that actually happen?" or words to that affect!

Yet more heavy touring ensued, including a series of sold-out shows in Australia while demoing songs from their yet to be released third album, work for which was slotted in between tour dates. India was also revisited during this time.

It proved to be another four year gap between albums but the wait was more than worth it.

Asymmerty (2013) is an album which heads down the prog road even further than its predecessor while maintaining the prog/metal approach familiar to many.

On its release it charted at #1 in the ARIA Album Charts and *Karnivool* even received an ARIA award. Many Australian bands have an aversion to the ARIA awards with *Midnight Oil* in particular voicing their disapproval of the awards. There is some feeling that *Karnivool* are of a similar mind.

The Refusal had received heavy rotation on radio through 'triple j' while enjoying several outings in live concert long before the album's release and was, therefore, known among fans. Perhaps it is the reason many cite it as the best track but it does have plenty of competition.

Asymmetry as a whole is not greatly represented by *The Refusal* as it draws away from the general progressive elements featured on many of the other tracks. It is heavier than most and I feel, without fear of contradiction, would have sat well on *Themata*. Even after several listens to this album I still can't go past *Sound Awake* as the way to introduce anyone to *Karnivool*.

As of the time of writing (2021) we still await a fourth album which was rumoured to appear during 2020. As we all know 2020 was the 'year from hell'. Tours were cancelled and re-scheduled tours were also cancelled with no sign at this stage when touring (or life) will return to normal.

It may also seem odd that only three albums have been issued over such a long period but one should keep in mind that all members of the band are tied into 'other projects' with some running in tandem with the activities of *Karnivool.*

Most popular here in Australia are *Birds of Tokyo* who are described as alternative and include vocalist *Ian Kenny.* They are a popular touring attraction and have even played at AFL (Australian Football League) games as half-time entertainment. One such event was the annual Anzac Day game – Anzac's are the soldiers from Australia and New Zealand who fought together during the Great War – and drew disapproval from veterans - not due to the music but rather their name.

I am not a fan and therefore will not dwell any further on the band or its output. Suffice to say that *Ian Kenny* was with the band prior to *Karnivool* and continues to be so.

Personally I was drawn to an album by a band called *Floating Me* – mentioned in the previous chapter – and as promised I will elaborate.

Jon Stockman was approached to add bass parts and is the reason why it drew my interest as I have made no secret of my love of the instrument and his playing style. He was available due to his parent band allowing *Ian Kenny* time out for his work with *Birds of Tokyo.*

Floating Me (2011) moves in a more progressive style than either *Karnivool* or *Birds of Tokyo* and is often cate-gorised as alternative. They probably come close to the *Church* but somewhat heavier without being considered overtly metal or prog/metal.

The band are made up of ex-members of *Scary Mother* and *Cog* and on this, their only album to date, the line-up is; *Andrew Gillespie* (lead vocal), *Anthony Brown* (guitars), *Tobias Messiter* (keyboards), *Jon Stockman* (bass) and

Lucius Borich (drums). *Borich* left the band in 2012 but they are still considered a going concern.

They didn't set the charts alight but produced a superb album which was nominated for an ARIA award in the 'Hard Rock/Heavy Metal' category.

The latest news on *Karnivool* indicates that touring is to recommence with some European gigs in 2022 and a new album is taking shape, so all that is possible is to ride out the storm and be patient.

Meantime pull out your *Karnivool* albums and enjoy listening to one of Australia's great prog/metal bands.

KETTLESPIDER
AND
MALCURA

ON A COLD AND overcast late autumn Sunday after-noon I made my way to Moorabbin (about 20 kilome-tres southeast of Melbourne, Victoria) for a pre-arranged meeting with two members from the band *Kettlespider* – or so I thought.

What transpired was both illuminating and disap-pointing. More on what happened later.

Kettlespider perform instrumentally in a prog/metal style, but that does the band an injustice as their music is more expansive than the limitations that the descriptor might suggest.

I purchase (almost) all my music – high street record stores are all but extinct – on-line these days. This gives me time to browse and then research anything of interest, prior to purchasing. I would hardly be the only person doing so!

During one of these excursions I came across, what proved to be, *Kettlespider's* second full-length studio album *Kettlespider* (2017).

I was intrigued with the cover art which depicted a metallic like spider drawn on a stark white background. After reading some reviews in various forums I made my purchase.

The line-up was; *Geoffrey Fyfe* (keyboards), *Scott Ashburn* (guitars), *Colin Andrews* (bass) *Haris Boyd-Gerny* (guitars) and *Simon Wood* (drums/percussion).

My first impressions were confirmed after one listen and I commenced seeking further releases and information about the band.

Things proved more difficult than I'd imagined. Firstly, their website looked almost abandoned with quite a period of time since the last update. Secondly, the music was available in down-load only (I'm tactile and old fashioned – need the physical product). Lastly, it was apparent that just the two full-length studio albums were available.

Undeterred I went back on-line shopping and discovering *Avadante* (2012) bought it immediately.

Here are two well-crafted and musically proficient albums by a local band who had released them five years apart and nothing further to be found – anywhere!

When researching material for this book I decided to contact some of the prog musicians in Australia and through the website made enquiries regarding *Kettlespider*.

To my surprise *Simon Wood* responded and after some email exchange he informed me that he and *Colin Andrews* were playing at Moorabbin on Sunday 18th April 2021. If I was able to attend they would set aside some time to answer whatever questions I had.

Marvellous, I thought, so I duly typed out all my questions in readiness only to receive another email the night before saying, "by the way the band is called *Malcura*".

This news prompted a mad dash to the computer for some serious searching and the results proved illuminating indeed.

So let's return to Moorabbin. After having difficulty finding a parking space I eventually arrived at the venue – which turned out to be a food, wine and music venue with an outside area for the band.

The band had already set-up and were tuning-up for a three set stint over the next three hours. I sat watching and observing the three musicians – *Josh Voce* (guitar), *Colin Andrews* (bass) and *Simon Wood* (drums). Simon soon looked in my direction and mouthed my name. I confirmed with a 'thumbs-up'.

A few minutes later we were in conversation and I was introduced to *Colin* and *Josh* but time was not on our side as they needed to have a band talk and make ready to perform.

Malcura are described as 'flamenco/metal' or 'rock-meets-flamenco'. I have a preference for the latter.

Unsure of what to expect I sat as they ran through their first set and was entranced by the musicianship and utterly surprised by the music itself, which I found myself enjoying.

Josh Voce happened to be celebrating his 30th birthday that day and a large contingent of family and friends turned up to make sure he did just that.

Josh has a very Brian May/Ken Hensley look. Long 'cork-screw' black hair. More importantly he is quite a virtuosic guitarist and played a semi-acoustic. He also plays with local 'death metal' band *Annihilist* who released an EP *Vol 1* (2015).

Colin Andrews is a bassist with a beautiful melodic touch. He played a locally acquired custom made instrument by 'Shub' which is "a rare and wonderful piece indeed" according to *Simon Wood*. His preference however is Fender. He is quietly unassuming but lively when engaged in conversation.

Simon Wood sat behind a 'reduced' kit and later told me "I feel like Ringo". He may feel like Ringo but has more than passing resemblance to a very young Phil Collins (even with his playing style). As I was to discover he also has that 'Cheeky Chappie' persona associated with Phil Collins.

During their second set my wife, Louise, arrived and after some ten minutes remarked "They don't sing". "Nor do *Kettlespider*" I informed her.

When the second set finished I approached *Simon* and asked if he would spare a few minutes as we had to make our way home.

He and *Colin* joined us and also Colin's mother, who was in deep conversation with Louise.

My first question was, "Does this mean *Kettlespider* are defunct?"

Simon, more-or-less, confirmed they are. "We do talk about getting together again or forming a completely new band".

We chatted for a while regarding influences and equipment. Dream Theater is a big influence on most of the band.

"Portnoy" confirmed *Simon* "is an immense influence with all his diverse projects with the exception of 'Flying Colors'", which he thought was just okay. "Alan White and Bill Bruford are influences too. They are both unique and original and are able to manipulate the rhythms and poly-rhythms in creative ways".

His kit preference is Pearl but today he was playing his 'Ringo-sized' Ludwig kit.

Colin too has been influenced by John Myung and we both agreed that we'd never seen anyone else play with the speed and dexterity of JM.

I was then introduced to *Colin's* mother and informed that *Kettlespider* often rehearsed in her home. Every band should have such supportive parents!

This led to finance talk and both said the band hardly made any money and what they did make went on making albums and buying equipment. The lack of money and the devastating year of 2020 basically spelt the end of the road. *Colin* told me he actually makes money playing with *Malcura* and "that never happened with *Kettlespider*".

Simon possesses a great deal of knowledge regarding seventies prog and is also a self-confessed "Australian prog historian".

Unfortunately time was not of the essence and we shook hands with *Simon* extending an invitation to get in touch if I needed more information. "I will", I told him, and Louise and I left as the band prepared for their final set.

Kettlespider formed in 2011 and describe themselves as "A majestic and sometimes terrifying 5-legged beast", the name was derived after seeing a spider (the large huntsman spider often make their way in-doors) in the kettle at their old school music studio.

The line-up; *Geoffrey Fyfe* (keyboards), *Scott Ashburn* (guitars), *Colin Andrews* (bass) *Haris Boyd-Gerny* (guitars) and *Simon Wood* (drums/percussion), remained stable throughout their history.

Avadante (2012) is a concept album which received much attention and critical acclaim from publications such as 'PROG' and was featured heavily on 'Progarchives' forum and voted into the top 100 releases for 2012.

I, personally, have a preference for their first release and consider it a measured prog album rather than prog/metal.

Concept albums with lyrics are (sometimes) hard to fathom, concept albums without lyrics might be considered impossible to fathom. The music needs to convey the mood.

The cover art for *Avadante* combined with the track titles makes for an easy task as the music eloquently interprets the message. The male patient lying in a hospital bed is in a coma and all manner of strange things are going on around him, such as the demonic presence behind the bed. All is not lost though. An angelic figure outside the window with her hand penetrating (without shattering) the glass, offers hope of renewed life.

The album opens with a short *Introduction* – mainly sound-scapes – before *Discovery* welcomes one with a nod to Dream Theater and some Genesis style keyboards. Whereas the influences are not surprising they do not dominate. The musicianship of all five members of the band is virtuosic and conveys the feeling of our protagonist coming to terms with his predicament.

Avadante is a beautiful track full of complexity mixed with riffs and melodic moments to savour. Guitar passages are omnipresent and the bass melodic. Drums are solid and sometimes busy with keyboards under-stated but essential for the atmosphere created.

Comatose slows things down considerably with both acoustic and electric guitar. It is dream-like in places, befitting the title. It never becomes too heavy but does portray a feeling of helplessness that the protagonist was obviously experiencing, ending with plaintive piano.

Revelations is a title which speaks for itself, whether the patient is being subjected to realities from his life or experiencing the possibility of change is up to the listener to interpret. The music is evocative but powerful, in particular the drums and bass guitar. Some 'time-signature' changes are detectable and again the music is complex.

New Eyes – a short track – conveys hope for our protagonist that his dire situation is not terminal or permanent.

Reflections - is an epic and the longest track, commencing slowly with guitar and keyboards and building until some heavy drumming, riffs and bass break-out. Things slow a little before the track and album drift to a conclusion with sound effects and what sounds like magpies and human footsteps. Our protagonist's recovery is complete.

For a debut album *Avadante* is amazingly good – if short (under 35 minutes) – and received great reviews from many in the prog fraternity with the hope the band would continue for some time to come. As a concept it was a welcome change to find one's own meaning and I believe mine is not too far off the mark.

Five years is a substantial gap between albums, especially for a new band, particularly given the over-whelming reception of their debut, this gap, in hindsight, may appear a misjudgement.

The band was not idle by any means and had indeed hit the touring circuit with gusto. For instance, they toured their home state of Victoria during 2013 and recorded two singles (*The Transcent* and *Inevitable*). These two singles received release in the form of a live ep *Live at Black Pearl* (2014). Currently, from my research, this is only available on down-load from the official website. It is worth seeking out though, as it highlights the musicianship of *Kettlespider* in a live setting.

The band played Australia's Progfest (a series of festivals held around the country – Melbourne, Sydney and Brisbane – during January and celebrating its 10th anniversary in 2019 – several times.

In 2016 Adelaide, South Australia held the 'Vision Festival' which *Kettlespider* head-lined.

All the touring and great reviews saw them draw a loyal fan-base (not only in Australia) but in Europe and Japan and ensure the legacy of the band will continue, regardless what the future holds.

'Building a Spider' was a project under-taken during 2017. The project covered eight months with each month dedicated to one song (or 'leg'). After each song was completed it was released as a single. By October the whole project was completed with recording taking place in Victoria and production and mixing by band members *Geoffrey Fyfe* and *Simon Wood*. Released world-wide on 24th October *Kettlespider* (2017) received glowing reviews from 'prog' fans – mainly from Europe, Japan and America. Featuring heavily in magazines and forums in Europe and America the band appeared to be moving forward.

When I asked *Simon Wood* about the project his look conveyed more than any words although he indicated it would not be a "venture that would be repeated". *Colin Andrew's* nodded tacit agreement.

Kettlespider (2017) is conceptual insofar as the project 'Building a Spider' is concerned but the eight tracks stand-alone – except for *Break the Safe pt I and pt II.*

The Climber opens busily and a full-on band track which is relatively short.

Circus, on the other hand, highlights various band members' strengths with drum, bass, keyboards prominent and soaring guitar riding atop. Hard to define as metal (per se) but elements are to be found. It is melodic and enthralling.

Samsara opens acoustically before the rest of the band kick-in with some heavy drumming dominating. Again the soaring guitar rides high. This track is a little heavier.

Break the Safe pt I runs the gamut of styles with some heavy riffs on display in a Pink Floyd (circa The Wall) vein. The guitar is clearly the dominate instrument of this driving track.

Anubis gets under way with repeated drum beats. This track indicates more than any other why the prog/metal tag has been attached to *Kettlespider*, although it does have some quiet moments around the two-and-a-half minute mark, which I can only describe as similar to King Crimson (first incarnation). Heavy riffs propel the music prior to some subtle keyboard colouring and a (flamenco flavoured!) guitar. The guest trumpeter is more detectable here than on *Circus*.

Life has a very atmospheric and short opening before Simon Wood pounds his drum kit to life (or beats it to death!). Some very rhythmic guitar soloing is accompanied by a consistent bass throbbing away. It concludes with a full on metal sound.

Rebirth is, in my opinion, the stand out track from this set and the heaviest. There is, what appears to be, some interplay between guitar and keyboards – all kept in-line by excellent drumming.

Break the Safe pt II the last 'leg' of the project and if the band were rushing to finish things off by this time it is not apparent.

The opening sequence has a certain 'Yes' feel to it and the bass is on display to greater effect than on any other track. It is a track that drifts (not aimlessly) while still delivering some solid music. Around the two minute mark the guitar betrays the Dream Theater influence and maintains it until the end.

What does the future hold for the band?

Haris Boyd-Gerny has returned to teaching, albeit in music, and appears, Simon informs me, "happy with his decision".

Geoffrey Fyfe is (at present) living and working in Liverpool, England as an audio-engineer.

Scott Ashburn builds guitars for Maton.

As for *Simon Wood* and *Colin Andrews* the answer is obvious. They are together in *Malcura* and, from my observations, enjoying themselves.

It is patently obvious, given the release dates that the two bands were running in tandem for some time and this may well explain the long gap between their two albums.

Malcura

The original line-up for *Malcura* was; *Josh Voce* (guitars), *Steven 'BV' Angell* (guitars) and *Simon Wood* (drums and percussion), in fact both their albums have the same line-up.

Their first self-titled album *Malcura* (2016) clearly indicates and over-lapping between the band and *Kettlespider,* in fact it was engineered and mastered by *Geoffrey Fyfe.*

Musically it is a major departure for all three (coming from prog/metal and death metal backgrounds) but obviously, from my observations, one they really enjoy.

The album cover is glorious depicting the band name on what resembles a tombstone amid encroaching undergrowth.

In retrospect I wish I had spent some time with *Josh Voce* but what little time I had with him was pleasing and he graciously stepped aside as I talked with *Simon Wood* and *Colin Andrews.*

As suggested earlier the music is heavily flamenco based with *Josh's* acoustic guitar high in the mix and dominant but not over-riding the other musicians. It should also be considered that both their albums to date do not have a bass player. Obviously the configuration of the band I saw was a more recent idea.

Linear notes indicate that *Black Cloud Float Pt:4* was performed by *Simon Wood,* but no such track is listed, however there is a 'Pt:3' which is mainly acoustic guitar and drumming. That said, the track ends at 5'22" and silence ensues for some 30 seconds before keyboard effects enter and take the track to its conclusion – perhaps this is 'Pt:4"!

A serendipitous discovery I am happy to add to my collection.

Simon and *Colin* enthused about honing their music as buskers in Bourke Street Mall, Melbourne and mainly due to the response they decided to carry it further. Gigs were often fulfilled in the most unlikely of settings and once saw the band perform on a catamaran in Cooktown, Queensland!

Malcura II (2020) continues along much the same lines as their debut but electric guitar is more apparent. Also appearing are guest musicians, *Fabian Acuna* and *Sarah Miller* – trumpet and flute respectively. Additionally 'scat' vocal by *Simon Wood* is apparent too.

This is an improvement on their debut and contains much of the music I saw them perform on the day.

City of the Moon Pt:2 is, apparently, a hidden track featuring *Simon Wood* and *Fabian Acuna.* I can only say it must be well hidden as I have yet to find it!

Malcura intend to extend the band to a four-piece (the three original members plus *Colin Andrews)* and I, for one, look forward to the release of an album featuring the four musicians.

There are plans to perform, in Melbourne, later this year (2021), in celebration of the release of *Malcura II* – complete with horn section. That will be worth seeing and an invite has been extended to yours truly.

All that remains for me to say is "thank you to both *Simon Wood* and *Colin Andrews* for their time and *Josh Voce* for his patience".

Malcura are from L to R Josh Voce, Simon Wood and Colin Andrews – by kind permission of Simon Wood

THE MERLIN BIRD

MELBOURNE BASED *THE MERLIN Bird* are a unique progressive rock band, encompassing elements of folk, rock, classical and Celtic influences – all of which make for an intriguing sound unlike anything I had experienced previously.

For sure, they have their influences such as Jethro Tull and indeed *Geoffrey Dawes* – mainstay and driving force behind the band – considers himself to be a big 'Tull' fan.

While sifting through a new delivery of discs during the early 2000's (while working at the Australian Broadcasting Corporation in the Sound Library) I came across the debut ep *Reason and Rhyme – The Merlin Bird* (2003). I have always been drawn by the cover art and so it was with this CD.

It is a fascinating blend of folk (with a Celtic influence), acoustic rock, classical overtones and progressive leanings. They describe themselves "as being like *Pink Floyd* meeting a bad-tempered *Enya* in an Irish pub, as sung by classically trained singers who have somehow ended up in a rock band that listens to *Genesis*" How does one get their head around that!?

The website biography continues to display informative and amusing offerings, such as the line-up "In order of height and presumed sanity, *The Merlin Bird* are: *Teleri Holton* (vocals), *Geoff Dawes* (keyboards, guitar, vocals), *Richard Allison* (keyboards and sense of humour) and *Dan Moloney* (drums, percussion and abstract irony). They are aided and abetted from time to time by singer *Beck Sian,* who is a cousin once removed to rock legend *Kate Bush,* and sounds like it"

The title track opens proceedings with atmospheres accompanied by a certain Celtic sounding instrumentation before the vocals arrive with a folk delivery and female backing in a classical mode. Although mainly acoustic an electric guitar adds some subtle nuances.

The calm before segues into *The Father of Storms* with dual male/female vocal. The latter bearing a remarkable resemblance to *Kate Bush.*

Puccini Garden is, unsurprisingly, classical in feel with beautiful reed instruments and keyboards and purely instrumental. Around the one minute thirty point the underpinning of bass and drum make an appearance and carry the piece to its conclusion.

Beholder's Eye reverts to the Celtic feel, particularly vocally. Lyrically it is about a group of friends enjoying a final drink in the pub before parting company and complimenting each other – the sort of thing that happens when one has a little 'too much' and reveals their more inner feelings.

Reason to Rhyme reverses the wording of the title track and relatively short in duration (1.26), it is a 'reprise' of the title track and bookends the disc very nicely.

Searching in vain for a full-length follow-up proved fruitless and after a few years I just stopped looking, until considering content for this book.

I decided to contact the band through their website as to all-intents-and-purposes they appeared to still be a going concern. Eventually I was put in touch with *Geoffrey Dawes* who proved extremely helpful and very encouraging.

What follows is a 'covid' remote Q and A which was to throw light on *The Merlin Bird* history and activity during the almost twenty years since their debut ep.

Q. Your live performances sound amazingly good entertainment. Would you elaborate and perhaps relate touring stories, particularly concerning '*Tull*'?

A. Ah, alas. We didn't tour with *Tull* as such – it was a one-off show at the Night of the Prog Festival in Germany in 2007, but we were stoked to be appearing on the same bill as *Jethro Tull, Asia* and other luminaries, as I'm sure you can imagine. It was an interesting one. If truth be told we weren't that settled as a band when we played the show – it was our fourth gig together with that line-up – and I think it showed. One of the audience members we spoke to afterwards said he thought we were better than Genesis (who had recently played their 'When in Rome' gig); high praise indeed, but not a view I felt able to share. Our guitarist *Dave* had a bit of a chat with *Ian Anderson* backstage, but otherwise the great man seemed to prefer keeping to himself.

It was an interesting insight actually, into how hard it must be to be everyone's hero. It must get wearing when your fame follows you around and doesn't leave you any room to just enjoy the day. The success that so many of us strive for has its price.

The earlier *Merlin Bird* shows were a lot of fun. Our bassist of many years – one *Dylan Stevenson* – was also a juggler, so I remember us putting together something that left him with both hands free so he could take the lead vocals and juggle.

Q. It is now fast approaching a further ten years between releases, anything in the pipe-line?

A. Yes indeed. We're currently writing for the next album, and although it will be our third release it actually feels a bit like a difficult second album syndrome. In some ways I think I've accumulated too many ideas; wrestling them all into coherent songs is the tricky bit.

Q. As I am also Melbourne based are there any plans to play live locally?

A. Not immediately, to be honest. The focus at this stage is getting the next album written and recorded, but the day will come, the day will come.

Q. You have listed the basic line-up, is it possible to offer some background on each member and perhaps why *Richard* is credited with 'sense of humour' and *Dan* with 'abstract irony'?

A. Ah, the 'sense of humour' and 'abstract irony' bits were largely my attempt to make the biography more interesting (and so in a small way, perhaps they worked). Okey dokey...

Dan Moloney: Feels like the heart of the band; the passion that somehow never dies. He played drums for a while with one of Melbourne's local songwriters, and people would come just to see him play. Unusually for a drummer he's also no slouch at keyboards and guitar. It makes him, I think, more sensitive in his drumming as he knows how it rolls from the other side of the kit.

Richard Allison: Is the musician of the band. He is a professional piano teacher, but also the prime mover behind *Entangled* – Melbourne's foremost Genesis tribute band. (Check them out – seriously worth a look!) I'm constantly amazed by how he can start with a musical theme and then take it to amazing places that no-one ever saw coming.

Teleri Holton: the voice of the band now for some years, she was (and is) a Renaissance-style singer. In this I suppose she continues the grand *Merlin Bird* tradition of us never having a female vocalist who is primarily a rock singer. T comes from a musical family and it shows. (She has a weird notation when writing her musical parts that I completely fail to understand, but it seems to make perfect sense to her.)

Geoff Dawes: and as for myself, you asked what my background was. Apart from progressive rock – my first musical love – I also performed through the 1990's in a series of musical theatre roles, including Gilbert & Sullivan and other shows of varying modernity. That exposure to different musical styles was really helpful when it came to my own writing, but it really all started when I got hold of the *Genesis* album *Wind and Wuthering* in my early teens. It doesn't always get the recognition it might, but I still see that one as a master-class of song-writing. I took up guitar and reintroduced myself to piano on the strength of that album, because one day I wanted to write songs like that. (Still trying.)

Q. *Beck Sian* sounds interesting with her background. I'm a 'totally smitten' Kate Bush fan. A little more would be great.

A. *Beck* is one out of the box. We met when I answered an ad she had left on the noticeboard of the local milk bar in Tecoma in the Dandenongs, near where we both lived. I was after a singer to help with backing vocals on the first CD, and kind of won the lottery when the person on the other end of the ad was *Beck.* Apart from being a wonderful person with an extraordinary freedom of musical expression, what are the chances that the person who placed a milk bar ad would share *Kate Bush's* family vocal chords? *Beck* put on a tribute night to *Kate* some years ago, and I was able to help out on keyboards for a couple of songs. She showed some pictures from the family album, including shots of *Kate* visiting *Beck's* family home in the foothills of the Dandenongs. I was a totally smitten KB fan myself, but never realised she'd been trapezing around within 10 minutes of where I grew up.

I later made comment in an email about the *Genesis* album *Wind and Wuthering* and how I missed *Steve Hackett's* input to the band. "Yep" replied *Geoff* "you're not wrong about missing Steve Hackett!

(Although a generation of pop fans – and a few record company execs – may sadly disagree.)"
Chapter and Verse (2014) proved to be the follow-up to *Reason and Rhyme* and again, the cover art appealed to me

The group of performers listed for the album are; *Geoff Dawes* and *Dan Moloney* (vocals, keyboards, guitars, drums, percussion and human noises), *Dave O'Toole* (guitars), *Trevor Carter* (electric guitar) and *Ross Kroger* (bass).

Listed as *Chapter of Choristers* are; *Shakira Searle, Beck Sian, Teleri Holton, Jessica Nabb* and *Dylan Stevenson.*

Prologue: To the Unknown God, is nothing short of amazing and veers away from the prominent Celtic feel of their debut. Following is *Introduction: Chapter and Verse* which is voice and piano driven and just glorious.

Chapter: 3 is an extremely short interlude (17 seconds) and led some to comment, on various forums, that *The*

Merlin Bird appear to be – considering the album thus far – a Christian band. The following two short tracks seemed only to add to the presumption.

When I mentioned this to *Geoff* his reply was mixed with surprise and a little understanding of how some arrived at the notion of Christianity.

"We're not, and I was actually a bit surprised that people made that association based on (I gather) nothing more than the title of our second CD. That said, there are certainly biblical themes running through there, but I've always dabbled in that side of things as part of a wider interest in human spirituality and psyche."

The only album I can possibly compare this to is *Enigma 2 – The Cross of Changes* (1993). Playing both back-to-back is quite revealing.

The album continues in much the same vein with the *Choristers* to the fore and sounding superb.

To pick out some personal highlights proved a little difficult as I found myself with too many and had to narrow the list down. Eventually I picked three – one of which I have already commented on, which is the opening track.

The Turning has a more rock/folk feel with driven piano and singular male vocal. The drumming is more than beat-keeping but not a showy display. Some eastern-style instrumentation is detectable and all-in-all it is a track which enjoys high rotation.

Another Story Told is the longest and most epic sounding and close to my choice of 'best on album'. Again, piano is prominent with the same male vocal although excellent backing vocal punctuated throughout. The drums are at times 'regal' and 'heralding' – hardly musical terminology but I am not a musicologist and therefore have my own way to describing the sounds I hear. Finally one can hear some under-stated electric guitar, with just the slightest tinge of blues.

The whole wonderful album ends with the short *to be continued...?* I look forward to that.

As mentioned previously the band are currently working on their third (or difficult second album syndrome) album. The difference between their two recordings to date is fairly stark with the debut displaying a greater Celtic influence to the latter.

During another communiqué with *Geoff* concerning the supposition that *The Merlin Bird* are a Christian band he told me; "I wrote (rather over-ambitiously) a twenty-something minute piece in high school based on the Tibetan mystic Milarepa. (In retrospect it was largely rubbish, but I handed it in for an English project and the kind teacher gave it an A-minus. Probably didn't want to break my young and sensitive heart.)"

I wonder if he has ever considered revisiting the piece with the hind-sight and experience garnered since would it be possible to turn it into a 'concept' album or just an epic track. Either way it would be interesting to get into the mind of a young *Geoff Dawes*.

I wish to extend my thanks to *Geoff* for his time, patience, encouragement and his kind permission in reproducing the album covers for inclusion in this, relatively, short chapter. It would be a pleasure to one day meet him in person and enjoy the experience of seeing *The Merlin Bird* live.

not
DROWNING,
WAVING

NOT DROWNING, WAVING FIRST came to my attention in the very early 1990's while watching a documentary on the ABC concerning Australia's involvement in Papua New Guinea. The musical back-drop leapt out at me and I just had to know who composed and performed it. When the programme finished I sat transfixed watching the copious credits roll by waiting for the music credit. Alas, there wasn't any indication whatsoever. Un-deterred I made note of the programme name with date and time of transmission and phoned the television station the following day. I was put through to the 'Sound Library' – little did I know within a few short years I would be working there – and the person I spoke with was unaware of the programme but jotted down my name and number and promised to get back to me. "Yeah, sure, I thought" but within a short period of time they did just that and informed the music was taken from an album called *Tabaran* (1990) by *Not Drowning, Waving*. Thus began a wonderful musical journey with one of Australia's hidden treasures.

Formed in Melbourne circa 1983 by *David Bridie* and *John Phillips* they incorporated rock, ambient and world music elements to lyrical themes mainly based on Australian experiences and concerns. Their history is punctuated with long periods of inactivity (including a break-up lasting around seven years) but nonetheless produced nine full-length studio albums, two of which were soundtracks for Australian films involving actor *Russell Crowe*. Also running concurrently during the last three years of their first incarnation was the side project *My Friend the Chocolate Cake (MFTCC)*, an acoustically based pop spin-off involving members of the parent band.

I quite liked *MFTCC* but will not include their catalogue as their music does not, in my opinion, fall into the parameters of this book.

David Bridie and *John Phillips* released albums under their own names as a collective and also solo. I will include a couple of *Bridie's* solo albums at the end as his solo work mirrors *Not Drowning, Waving* rather than *MFTCC*.

The band name was taken from the poem *Not Waving but Drowning* by English poet *Stevie Smith* (1902–1971) and highlighted her macabre sense of humour. A collection of her poems was issued under the title of this – her most famous – poem.

The core of the band were; *David Bridie* (vocals, piano, keyboards), *John Phillips* (guitar), *Rowan McKinnon* (bass), *James Southall* (percussion) *Russel Bradley* (drums) *Helen Mountfort* (cello) and *Tim Cole* (tapes, vocals) although musicians were brought in to supplement individual tracks with often an additional two or more appearing on any given album. During their history some sixteen musicians participated on their albums and live performances.

They released a 'dance' single *Mr Pooh (Do be a don't be)* (1985) but it was hardly representative of the album from which it was lifted and did little or nothing to raise their profile. However it did indicate *David Bridie's* quirkiness which re-surfaced on subsequent albums.

Another Pond (1985) was their debut from which the single came. It is an album full of atmospheric ambience and effects with minimal or understated instrumentation, usually piano. *David Bridie's* often whispered wistful vocals dominate the non-instrumental tracks. It could almost pass for 'meditating' or mood music, with the exception of the aforementioned single. It does, however, point the direction in which they proceeded until the end of the decade. A later repressing, circa 1991, includes two re-worked tracks *Another Pond* and *Perfect Design* which included *Helen Mountfort* (cello, keyboards) who would prove 'instrumental' on future albums.

The Little Desert (1986) released almost a year on from their debut is more up-beat but only just. The opening track, *The Same Heat*, setting out their stall for what followed; atmospheres, piano and vocals the most dominate features. This track has the inclusion of cello by *Phillip Wale* which is just glorious. Cello appears on other tracks and saw the introduction of *Helen Mountfort* in the band.

Some tracks sound like they would not be out of place on a soundtrack album, in particular *Blackfish Creek* and *Wilma's Dream*, the latter featuring piano only.

Storm is a wonderful track and a clear indication of what the future held for fans willing to stay the course. The 'storm' and 'black Cockatoos' tape effects were recorded on location in Melbourne, Victoria by *Les Gilbert* and an obvious reference to this very Australian song.

A few tracks have just one, two or three members taking part with solo parts by *David Bridie* and *John Phillips*.

From my perspective this is an improvement on their debut.

Cold and the Crackle (1987) progressed even further from *The Little Desert* bearing all the hallmarks that were displayed on subsequent albums. The band had found their niche and developed a following. The appearance of seven core members plus eight guest musicians make this one of the most heavily populated albums in their catalogue.

These first three albums were retrospectively added to my collection after seeking out the previously mentioned

Tabaran – which I found in my favourite record store along with, what proved to be, their fourth studio album.

Claim (1989) proved pivotal for *Not Drowning, Waving*. Not just an amazing leap forward but, *Claim was* voted 'best Australian album' by *Rolling Stone* magazine's reader's poll. Personally, I consider it the best in their catalogue.

The album is brimming with references to Australian life and is altogether very up-beat displaying a growing confidence. The quirkiness is also in evidence during the instrumental track *Wobble* although there are vocal credits given to 'Bugs Bunny and Donald Duck'. They can be heard saying 'duck season, rabbit season, fire' – a very famous piece of dialogue from one of the cartoons.

Palau otherwise known as the Republic of Palau is an island country situated in the western Pacific. It has a chequered history including a 'free association' with the United States. It is this political situation on which the song is based. It receives a 'reprise' at the end with the '*Micronesian Mix*', which I prefer to the original.

Terra Nullius and *Claim* round out the album beautifully (prior to the 'reprise') with the latter incorporating the sound of the didjeridoo.

It is difficult to know if *David Bridie* pens his lyrics from experience or observation and one example stands out on the album. *Fishing Trawler* is performed by nine musicians with the inclusion of; viola, trumpet and trombone. The title speaks for itself and my guess would be it was written from observation. It is also my stand out track from a stand out album.

During 1988 *Not Drowning, Waving* visited Papua New Guinea where they met local musicians, including *George Telek*. This visit and meeting resulted in the album which first drew my attention to the band *Tabaran* (1990). The album is credited to *Not Drowning, Waving and the musicians of Rabaul, Papua New Guinea – featuring Telek.*

Telek appears on three tracks; the title track, *Pila Pila* and *Abebe,* the latter two as part of the ensemble *Moab Stringband.* Other tracks feature a variety of local singers and musicians. *Abebe* starts with a spoken introduction in pidgin-English – presumably from a radio broadcast.

As close to 'world music' as the band ever got it is an amazing diversion with its mix of local instrumentation and *Not Drowning, Waving's* 'western' influences. This is an album which is well worth your time exploring.

Tabaran was subsequently nominated for 'Best Indigenous Release' at the ARIA Awards in 1992.

Proof is an Australian 'cult' movie featuring; *Hugo Weaving, Genevieve Picot* and a very young *Russell Crowe. Weaving* plays the part of a 'blind from birth' photographer Martin, who is brought up by his mother. Living alone he requires the home-help and Celia, played by *Picot,* provides it along with amorous advances which are not welcomed.

By chance he meets a kitchen-hand Andy *(Russell Crowe)* and explains he takes photos as proof that what he senses is what others see. He engages his new friend to interpret his photography. There follows a series of adventures with some hilarious moments and some poignant moments too.

Proof (1992) is the accompanying soundtrack and is a mix of very ambient and minimalistic music with some film dialogue and all track titles consisting of one word (*walk, Sunday, sad, happy* and *panic)* to name just a few.

The film ranks highly in my personal viewing and during our severe lockdown of 2020 was watched at least twice! The soundtrack is a matter of personal taste.

Circus (1993) was their next 'proper' album and sits well with *Claim,* if a little more accessible and commercial.

Crazy Birds gets things under-way with the most commercially sounding track on the album with a 'catchy' – or at least as 'catchy' as *Not Drowning, Waving* ever achieved – chorus. It appears written from personal experience and contains aspects of growing up in Australia.

Teteko is a small town in New Zealand (Te teko) which is referred to as Texas by the locals. It paints a wonderful picture and is perhaps from personal experience during a visit by *David Bridie. Helen Mountfort* contributes some beautiful cello which is glorious.

There is, naturally, political comment throughout the entire album with outstanding tracks; *Slumber in Tumbleland, Albert Namatjira, Norman Young* and *Parish Pump.*

Albert Namatjira (1902–1959) was a pioneer of indigenous Australian art born in central Australia. He was born and raised at Hermannsburg Lutheran Mission, just outside Alice Springs. His western influenced water colours of outback Australia made him a household name and his pictures hung prominently in many homes. In 1957 he was granted Australian citizenship and freed from the restrictions associated with being a 'ward of the state' or 'stolen generation' depending on your viewpoint.

Obviously this is all touched upon in the song with compassion and a leaning toward the Indigenous telling of the story. Musically it mirrors much of *Not Drowning, Waving's* output with every member of the band (*Bridie, Phillips, Bradley, McKinnon, Mountfort* and *Southall*) contributing poignantly to this beautiful track.

Norman Young is an instrumental track but contains the subject in question 'speaking on life'. I have been unable to establish just who Norman Young was/is but his observations on life are of interest.

The Migrant and *Parish Pump* are observation tinged with political comment.

The album ends in sombre and reflective mood with *Walk me Home* and adds to the overall 'feel' of a superb addition to their catalogue.

It was in support of this album that I saw *Not Drowning, Waving* in a live context.

In 1994 the juggernaut that was *Peter Gabriel's Secret World Tour* rolled into Australia and Adelaide was where my daughter and I would catch this concert. Our tickets merely noted + support.

Rumour has it that *Gabriel* hand-picked *Not Drowning, Waving* as support and given his involvement with 'WOMAD (World of Music and Dance)' their direction and style would have appealed to him. *Peter Gabriel* personally introduced the band, extolling them as well worth coming in – a remark aimed at those still at the bar – to see.

Sadly his words evaporated among the beers and fast-food outlets dotted around and the arena was only about one third full. Of those left some absent-mindedly leafed through their programme while others chatted and only a small number sat attentively listening. Even after close to ten years into their career their profile was not high and quizzical looks from some were more than apparent.

I thoroughly enjoyed the whole experience and from memory (unable to attain a programme) the band was; *David Bridie* (vocals, keyboards), *John Phillips* (guitar, vocals), *Rowan McKinnon* (bass), *Helen Mountfort* (cello, strings), *Russel Bradley* (drums, percussion) and *James Southall* (percussion). Obviously much of *Circus* was performed and a fair smattering of their back-catalogue too.

1994 was also the year the band broke up. With most band members involved with *MFTCC* with its more acoustic pop approach they concentrated on building 'Chocolate Cake's' profile while *Bridie* and *Phillips*, in particular, also released solo albums.

Hammers (aka Hammers over the Anvil) (1994) was recorded in 1993 and proved the last album from the first incarnation of the band. Much like *Proof* before it, it was a soundtrack to an Australian movie involving *Russell Crowe*. The movie is a mostly forgettable tale of hero worship and infidelity but the music is wonderful and in keeping with the output of *Not Drowning, Waving*.

Bridie and Phillips collaborated on a few albums which mainly concentrated on music for film, stage and theatre while *Bridie* was more prolific as a solo artist and with *MFTCC*.

Not Drowning, Waving released an album in 2006 that appeared, at first, to be a new recording but, '*maps for sonic adventures*' proved to be an album of 17 remixed – or 'remapped' – tracks stretching across their catalogue. It is very interesting if not essential but one I personally enjoy listening to from time to time.

A number of one-off reunions over the years culminated in an appearance at the WOMADelaide festival in 2005 with special guest *Telek*.

David Bridie also appeared on albums by *Lior* and *Telek* but his solo work is the best of his many ventures and for that reason I will consider two of his albums.

Act of free Choice (2000) was his first 'real' solo venture with the title referencing an event arranged by the

Indonesian Government when West Papuan delegates were rounded up by the military and incarcerated until they agreed to vote on behalf of their fellow countrymen in favour of a republic.

From all the musicians associated with *Not Drowning, Waving* and *MFTCC* only a few appear on this album, most notably; *John Phillips, Helen Mountfort* and *Hope Cstoros.*

The Koran, the Ghan and a Yarn is the first track and it's difficult to grasp what it all means. The Ghan is one of the world's longest train journeys and runs from Adelaide to Darwin through the Northern Territories. It appears to be simply wordplay.

Not surprisingly a few tracks are reflective of his work with *Not Drowning, Waving* but none sound like *MFTCC.*

Salt (I don't want to go no further) is quirky and up-beat but certainly not overtly representative of the album, although it is a track which is both enjoyable and deviating.

My personal favourite is *Float* – which segues from and appears a continuation of *The Deserters* – is a drum and piano driven track with typical *Bridie* vocals and his plaintive exhortation to "let there be no more regrets".

Succumb (2008) prompted the author to review this much over-looked album on the Amazon forum under the moniker of 'prog is not dead'. It can hardly be consider plagiarism if I quote myself. So here is my very short review.

"Why *David Bridie* and for that matter *Not Drowning, Waving* have not had greater recognition or airplay is beyond belief.

This was his third solo venture but suffice to say he gathered a great bunch of musicians to interpret his ideas and sounds and what transpires is yet another exceptionally good recording from DB.

It's hard to pigeon-hole the man as he uses sonic soundscapes and writes amazingly thought provoking lyrics to his evocative music. Some may say he borders on the 'progressive', others may have differing opinions but no matter the end result is a thoroughly great album worthy of any category one wishes to put it in.

Very Australian in his outlook and writing *Bridie's* writing and music stand alone and more than a worthy addition to any serious music fan's collection."

Difficult to add anything further to my first reactions after listening to this gem of an album other than mention one of my favourite tracks.

The foreign correspondent was written for Mark Worth, an Australian journalist and documentary film maker who was found dead in his hotel room in Papua New Guinea on the 17th January 2004 in mysterious circumstances. His death is still under investigation. The lyrics were inspired by eulogies at his funeral.

Typical of *Bridie's* lyrical and musical style it also reconnects him with Papua New Guinea – albeit not the way he would have desired.

In conclusion, should any reader be unaware of *Not Drowning, Waving, MFTCC* or *David Bridie* and *John Phillips* then investing a little time researching the catalogues of all would, in my opinion, be time well spent. Happy hunting!

UNITOPIA SOUTHERN EMPIRE AND UNITED PROGRESSIVE FRATERNITY

UNITOPIA, SOUTHERN EMPIRE AND *United Progressive Fraternity* all have a common thread running through them which will be confirmed as we deal with each individually.

UNITOPIA

Adelaide based *Unitopia* were active from approximately 1996 to 2014 and formed by *Mark Trueack* (vocals) and *Sean Timms* (keyboards and guitar).

My research for this chapter could not reveal anything of significance from 1996 through to the independent release of their debut album *More than a Dream* (2005). Frustrated I began contacting the band through websites and sent a general enquiry through the *United Progressive Fraternity* website.

To my utter surprise, within a short space of time, *Mark Trueack* emailed to say "Let's talk on face-book". Not about to let this opportunity slip by I readily agreed but not being on 'face-book' appeared a stumbling block. Quickly rectifying that problem I made contact. Shortly *Mark* and I were in conversation then.....disconnected. A few seconds later he requested my mobile number and a long, interesting and diverse conversation ensued. The relevant parts of which will slowly find their way into the body of this chapter.

Suffice to say that the period between 1996 and 2005 was filled productively with various internal and external forces being brought to bear which held up release of their debut. First and foremost, *Mark* was still working as a record executive while *Sean* had created his own production company, *Timms Tunes* and composed music for advertising agencies and later recorded there with *Southern Empire.* Their partnership focused as a writing team.

Prior to their meeting *Trueack* had performed live, creating 'The Genesis Touch' in tribute to the band – something he returned to later for the 25th anniversary of *John Lennon's* death.

Mark 'Truey' Trueack, as he is affectionately known to fans has often referred to the fans as 'fellow Unitopians'. He is concerned about a number of issues regarding this planet we share and feels music with a message can reach people who may not otherwise be informed.

Unitopia created some amazing music in their time but that gap between the initial meeting of *Trueack* and *Timms* and the release of their first album is not so puzzling when one knows all the circumstances.

"I didn't want any conflict of interest with the release of our album" says *Mark.* That 'conflict' was the fact he worked as an executive for EMI and sought out other labels on which to release their albums.

They started the writing of their debut which would be independently released and receive a further revamped release in 2017 by 'Giant Electric Pea'.

I was introduced to *Unitopia* through a good friend in Adelaide who sent copies of their first two albums, describing them as 'crossover prog'. I had a good listen before I decided to buy. Loving what I was hearing I made my way to a local record store but could only find the album *Artificial* (2010). This has become my favourite album but I was able to add the first two when they were re-released as box sets more recently. I consider *Unitopia* a symphonic progressive band exhibiting virtuoso playing but extremely accessible and lyrically deep and thought provoking.

More than a Dream – The Dream Complete (2017) was the product of *Mark* and *Sean* reuniting after a less than amicable breaking-up of *Unitopia* in 2014 but I'm jumping the gun and will elaborate later.

I have always enjoyed this album but should you not have a copy then I would strongly suggest purchasing this three disc set. Simply put it far surpasses the original as it contains bonus material and includes a new track written specially with this release in mind.

More than a dream is, of course, the title track but also a highlight among many highlights. One thing that 'grabbed' me straight 'off the bat' was *Trueack's* vocals and on this track they are sublime and coupled with contributions from the *Adelaide Art Orchestra* among others which lends the track a majestic feel. The guitar is also prominent and soars high in the mix to great effect.

One of the bonus tracks on disc one is *Unitopia* and its inclusion adds a new dimension to an already great debut but it's the other two discs which make this an essential purchase.

Disc two is remixes and re-workings but unlike much of their ilk it too is essential listening as these are done so well, sounding very different to the originals and at times has the feel of a new album.

Two amazing epics get things under way on disc three – in particular *The Decameron Day 6 Tale 9* in all its 20 plus minute glory. *Mark Trueack* has made no secret of their love for this amazing track and believes "it deserves to be heard". The disc also has a number of 'dance mixes' but I would defy anyone to dance to these! Concluding with a couple of unreleased demos which sound more like the finished article and, as previously mentioned, the new track *The Dream Complete*.

Live work would soon be taken up with greater urgency with the album being launched at the 'Cavern Club' in Adelaide – wonder where that name came from!

The album received an international release in 2006 through the Canadian label Unicorn Records.

To complete the line-up Adelaide artists; *Matt Williams* (guitar/vocals), *Monty Ruggiero* (drums), *Shireen Khemiani* (bass) and *Tim Irrgang* (percussion) were recruited and *Trueack* and *Timms* got down to the serious business of writing a new album.

Prior to the release of their next album *Unitopia* signed a three album deal with the progressive label 'InsideOut'. They also complimented the core line-up with; *Mike Stewart* (saxophones), *Amanda Timms* (flute), *Kiki Celarik* (vocals) and an eight piece string section *The Amicus Strings*.

The result of all this activity saw fruition with the release of *The Garden* (2009) a double CD spanning approximately 100 minutes of pure symphonic progressive rock music. It was re-released later as an expanded three disc box set in 2020. Again I urge those who do not have the album to shelve out a few extra dollars for the latter version as the extras on disc three are mainly live performances – presumably from the 'More than a Garden of Dreams' tour of Europe in 2010 – with an added new track *Tears from the Garden*.

The original recording appears on disc one and two and the remastering makes it another essential purchase for serious music listeners and received accolades from many in the prog community. Typical was 'Review Busters' calling it a "unique blend of progressive rock with some symphonic parts that are incredible", also stating it was "easy on the ears".

High praise and fully deserved in my opinion. This is indeed a 'treat' for any prog fan to enjoy time and again.

Slight changes occurred in the line-up with *Shaun Duncan* coming in on bass and upright bass, *Jamie Jones* (drums) plus special guests and the *Amicus Strings* supplementing the band on their next recording – which was released within a year of *The Garden.*

Artificial (2010) is and remains an album I personally have on high rotation at home, regarding it as the best from an outstanding catalogue.

Although the ten tracks can individually 'stand-alone' it is clear this album was always intended to flow like a suite and is in fact referred to as *Artificial Suite.* To fully enjoy this 'presentation' of modern prog it is necessary to listen from start to finish. *Mark Trueack's* thought provoking lyrics give added weight to the music, in particular with the 'reimagining' in 2019.

There is a reoccurring musical and lyrical themes throughout with beautiful references to *the Beatles* songs; *Come Together* and *Fool on the Hill,* also featuring some swooping strings and Beatle-esque motifs.

Over the next couple of years as work progressed on, what proved to be, their last album the relationship between *Trueack* and *Timms* was suffering and resulted in the dissolving of *Unitopia* by 2014.

"I love *Sean* like a brother", says *Mark* during our phone conversation and even though *Timms* was to say they would never work together again this proved not to be the case – as we shall see.

One Night in Europe (2011) is a document of the bands European tour from the previous year and includes tracks from all three studio albums including the amazing *Artificial Suite*. It was recorded at *Boerderij, Zoertermeer, Netherlands* – a venue solely existing to support progressive music – and the sound is brilliant. It is an understatement to call this a worthwhile addition – it is an essential addition from a band at their peak playing sublimely to a very appreciative audience.

Covered Mirror Vol.1. – Smooth as Silk (2012) is, as the title suggests, a covers album containing 'a selection of songs that inspire *Unitopia*' although it does present some new music. The title also beggared the question if a volume two was ever in the pipeline. "There was never a volume two" *Mark* informed me. It seemed the original idea was to release a double disc with the second sub-titled '*Hard as Rock*'. This may be when things got uneasy between them, although managerial problems did little to help the situation.

The album selection may surprise some with the inclusion of; *Calling Occupants of Interplanetary Craft* and *Everybody's got to learn Sometime* – the former by seventies 'enigma' band *Klaatu* and later covered by *the Carpenters* giving them a world-wide hit single. Most are familiar prog staples from the likes of; *Marillion, Genesis, Supertramp, Yes* and *Alan Parson's Project. Man of Colours,* a song by Australian pop band *Icehouse* is absolutely amazing. Should I have been asked to select one of their songs it would have been this one – they were more than the average eighties pop band.

Sean Timms formed *Southern Empire* while *Mark Trueack* together with some 'fellow *Unitopians*' formed the collective *United Progressive Fraternity*.

SOUTHERN EMPIRE

Among his many talents *Sean Timms* owns his own post production company – *Timms Tunes* – and is 'hand's-on'. He is an engineer, composer, arranger and producer aside from being an amazing keyboardist. He played piano from an early age but took great interest in synthesizers after his father bought him a copy of *Journey to the centre of the Earth* (1974) by *Rick Wakeman*.

The Gargoyle and other short stories (2008) is a presentation of the orchestral music of *Sean Timms* which (as yet) I have been unable to track down a CD copy of. It is, however, available on download.

After the demise of *Unitopia Sean Timms* began gathering like-minded musicians together to realise and bring to life his vision for *Southern Empire*. He had a long friendship with *Danny Lopresto* and had indeed suggested previously that they form a band of their own. Both agreed and sought other musicians from the Adelaide area.

The line-up for their first album was; *Danny Lopresto* (lead vocal and guitar), *Cam Blokland* (guitar), *Jez Martin* (bass), *Brody Green* (Drums) and *Sean Timms* (keyboards, vocals, saxophone and lap steel guitar).

All these musicians had 'tread the boards' for a considerable time and adept at various musical expression like jazz, metal and theatre. This made for a melding of styles and influences which would soon become evident.

It has been suggested that among their influences are the likes of; *IQ, Dream Theater, Transatlantic, Karnivool* and *Steven Wilson* – in his many guises, however their debut album also references *Unitopia,* which comes as no surprise as *Timms* credits *Trueack* in the genesis of some of the songs. It also appears that they had considered making it another *Unitopia* album but the aforementioned differences put paid to that idea.

Another connection is the inclusion of *Steve Unruh* (although not part of the core band) on their albums. He also joined *Mark Trueack* in *United Progressive Fraternity.*

Southern Empire (2016) became their self-titled debut and has a harder edged sound than *Unitopia* while maintaining all the prog accruements – great lyrics, melodies and virtuoso performances. They are heavier and even though *Mark Trueack* had some input the two bands are very different.

I eagerly awaited its release and purchased very early through the Amazon website.

The album opens with a very short (49 second) track *Show me the Way* which is mainly vocal sounding as though it is processed through an old radio with bad reception. It is however, part of the epic track which appears later.

Forest Fire kicks things off in earnest with thought provoking lyrics and the 'heavier harder edged sound' referred to earlier. It sets the scene for the album as a whole with superb playing and vocals from *Danny Lopresto,* who believes he is 'dirtier' than most prog vocalists. I prefer 'grittier' but a *Jon Anderson* or *James LaBrie* he certainly is not. He has a unique and appealing vocal displaying a harder and 'grittier' element.

How Long is a standout with keyboards reminiscent of *Rick Wakeman* – his father's purchase of '*Journey*' obviously made an impact on the young *Timms*. A certain jazzy feel also comes through with a beautiful sounding saxophone. It is, however, the next track which (for me) make this a sublime album.

The Bridge that binds is of epic proportions coming in at over 28 minutes and stands up with any epic from the modern prog era – and many from the past. This is when the opening sequence is expanded on and all becomes clear. *Mark Trueack* is credited with the 'idea' and it does have a little *Unitopia* feel in places.

Sean phoned *Mark* while working on the album and "was surprised I spoke with him" says *Mark*. Again *Mark* made it clear that he holds *Sean* in deep respect and is in awe of his talents. This setting aside of any past disagreements forged the way to remaster and re-issue in box set the first two *Unitopia* albums. Equally *Mark's* contribution to *Southern Empire* is there for all to hear on that epic track. *Sean Timms* is equally complimentary of *Trueack* in interviews.

The two also toured with a special acoustic band comprising members of; *Southern Empire, Unitopia, United Progressive Fraternity* and *Resistor* - the latter being a band for which *Steve Unruh* composed and played, which is still active as of 2021.

Southern Empire toured but only in their home state of South Australia – I'm unaware of them performing anywhere else in Australia – before setting out for Europe in 2018 in support of their second album. It would be reasonable to say that their profile is higher in Europe than at home. During the compiling of these short introductions I have mentioned the band to many friends to unresponsive stares

Civilisation (2018) was received exceptionally well with many touting it to be the 'prog album of the year'. I find it has more of a 'total band feel' than their debut which I believe is a natural evolution.

The 2018 tour also took in the *Boederoj, Zoetermeer, Netherlands* and is a venue I would love to get to but visits to relatives living in Holland have always been when no-one was touring and playing the venue. Alas, one day!

Civilisation comprises just four lengthy tracks with *Crossroads* another outstanding epic. The track has a bit of history harking back to *Unitopia* with *Trueack* credited in sleeve notes for some of the concepts but its total realisation here highlights a band straddling the gamut of influences and styles to amazing affect. If ever there was self-evident proof that *Southern Empire* is not a mark 2 version of *Unitopia* then here it is presented in its majestic sub 30 minute duration.

The opening track *Goliath's Moon* begins with a short extract of the old song '*By the light of the silvery moon*' performed by *Bill Murray and the Haydn Quartet* circa 1910. The booklet also quotes the then President of the United States famous words to astronaut Buzz Aldrin regarding the "priceless moment" when "all the people on this earth are truly one".

The other epic on the album is *Cries for the Lonely* which is lyrically thought provoking and musically brilliant. It is my personal favourite from a truly great album.

Innocence and Fortune close out an album that stands up to repeated listens with the band again jumping around many genres.

Rumours of a planned concept album have emerged which was believed to be ear-marked for 2020 release. We are well aware what that year brought to our lives and as of the time of writing no further news has 'leaked' to offer clues about the album or a potential release date.

Meanwhile, running in tandem with *Southern Empire* was *Mark Trueack's United Progressive Fraternity*.

UNITED PROGRESSIVE FRATERNITY

"Where are you?" asks *Mark Trueack* at the start of our telephone conversation. Telling him home is Victoria he offers his condolences! We have suffered more lock-downs and tighter restrictions than any other state in Australia and were currently in lock-down when we spoke. 'Yeah, it's a little hard", I say. "Bet you say that to all the boys" came the suggestive reply. If ever there was an ice-breaking moment *Mark* delivered it.

His intensified focus on our planet and its multitude of problems continues with *United Progressive Fraternity*. The aim is to bring together equally concerned musicians and make "interesting and meaningful musical arrangements". He does so with passion and integrity.

I suggested that not all prog collectives seemed to deliver great albums but that I felt *United Progressive Fraternity* sounded more like 'a band' rather than a collection of talented individuals, some of whom appeared more concerned that their contribution be as virtuosic as possible. "That's always been the aim" he assures me.

There is also a connection with *Samurai of Prog* (a core band plus many talented musicians) with *Steve Unruh* contributing in large measure to both bands.

Fall in love with the World (2014) saw *United Progressive Fraternity* quickly off the mark (if you'll pardon the pun). With some of progressive rock's luminaries getting involved and displaying a passion similar to *Trueack's* it was never going to be a show-case album for individual talent.

The title and opening track is a heart-felt plea to get involved and show some 'love' to the plight many find themselves in – often not of their own making but through environmental issues, climatic problems or war. It sets the scene for what follows and made a great impact with many prog fans. Just hope the message isn't obscured amidst all the brilliant music.

The list of artists is the proverbial 'who's-who' and includes; *Steve Unruh, Steve Hackett, Jerry Marotta, Colin Edwin, Chris Lebled, Jon Davison, Lisa Wetton* coupled with some names normally not associated with music such as; *Sir David Attenborough, Dame Jane Goodall, David Suzuki* – to name just a few.

Mark Trueack and *Steve Unruh* really are the driving force behind this project and together with *Christophe Lebled* are 'instrumental' in drawing in such large numbers of people to lend support and more.

Steve Hackett's contributions drew my attention as an old *Genesis* fan. When he left *Genesis* and started a solo career I followed him. It seemed natural that I ask "Did you actually record in the same studio as *Hackett?*" I suspected not but wanted it from the 'horse's mouth'. "No, it was all done by sending files back and forth" At least the pandemic has had one bonus for musicians around the world as they embrace new technologies and continue bringing fans satisfying music. I had missed out on seeing *Genesis Revisited* in 2020 due to Covid cancellations and mentioned I was looking forward to the rescheduled concert. "That won't happen" was *Mark's* considered opinion, one he did not elaborate on.

It needs to be admitted that I, after *Unitopia* disbanded, headed off in the *Southern Empire* direction, at least initially, as I saw *United Progressive Fraternity as* 'just another prog collective' – my big fat mistake!

The second album was not delivered until four years later but given the logistics of contacting and recording the different parts from the plethora of musicians that should come as no surprise. What eventuated is, in my opinion, one of the great albums of 2019 and deserving of a much wider audience on a number of levels.

Planetary Overload Part One: Loss (2019) has a sleeve depicting the many issues facing people and planet; pollution, war, environmental issues, even an individual wearing a mask and the 'doomsday clock' indicating five minutes to midnight.

The case opens out to reveal photos of those involved which amounts to around 60 people plus the *Fraternity Symphony Orchestra* conducted by *Cornel Wilczek*.

It doesn't take too much imagination to see why it took some time to coordinate and *Steve Unruh* and *Mark Trueack* display a passion and dedication which is staggering. Add to this the list of those thanked in the extensive booklet by both *Steve* and *Mark* and my admiration is immense.

The music is broken into three phases; *Dawning on Us, Distraction and Destruction* and *Growing,* with a combined duration of just under 75 minutes.

I have previously stated that *United Progressive Fraternity* sound more like a band than some other collectives I have heard. The cohesion and fluidity are evident and the music just glorious, again displaying thought provoking lyrics. It is difficult not to be overly effusive as I personally rate this album highly among the many I purchased during the last 18 months of 'pandemic on-line buying'.

As the television sales people say, 'but wait, there's more'.

A bonus disc featruing *Christophe Lebled, Mark Trueack* and *Steve Unruh* under the slightly unwieldy title *United Progressive Fraternity presents Romantechs: Reimagine.*

Romantechs appears to arrive from an album *Trueack* was working on with *Lebled* called *The Romantic.*

It contains nine previously recorded track which have, obviously, been 'reimagined' and presents an album which stands alone from *Planetary Overload* with some tracks from *Unitopia* being the highlight for me.

Fall in love with the World from the first album is amazing as is *This Time* but the final track *The Great Reward* from the *Artificial Suite* is just beautiful in this reimagined recording.

Mark Trueack has since been writing and composing with several things in the pipeline some of which reflect personal and painful experiences but it was his final remarks that hit home.

"I plan to release a solo album in 2023 – then retire and spend what time I have left with my wife". Read into that what you will but *Mark Trueack* has given so much plea-sure to so many over the years that one cannot deny him spending time with his family. I'm certain his passion and commitment will continue and should any feel inclined to offer support then I would encourage you to check out his website *unitedprogressivefraternity.com* – you will not regret it!

Finally a humble thank you from me to *Mark* for being generous with his time and encouraging with his remarks – not to forget all the wonderful music to enjoy.

...and OTHER SHORT STORIES

WHEN I WAS CONSIDERING this section initially, I thought to highlight three or four artists but ended up short-listing many more. Rather than omit any I shall write a little about each in the hope that you will appreciate and perhaps listen to what is on offer.

That I was unable to find too much information on any of these artists underscores the lack of media attention and interest in Australia toward the progressive and alternative genres. Artists who seem to gain most attention are those whose sound is heavier, leaning toward the metal genre – happily, that appears to include progressive metal.

Some of the following have released few albums. Some have, sadly, disbanded. Some are still making and releasing superb prog and some are fairly new to the scene with much still to contribute.

The long and arduous break from live music due to the coronavirus pandemic has also had an incredible impact on the capacity of many to record in the safe and welcoming studios they are accustomed to and remote file sharing has almost become the 'norm'.

Those who are able to 'get together' and exchange ideas are the lucky ones.

Writing without any idea of just when you can 'road test' the material has to be frustrating in the extreme. Fan reaction was always a barometer of how a song was progressing and the fine tuning was in response to that reaction. During this pandemic some artists have given us teasers on their Facebooks or websites and gauged reaction that way.

All-in-all it has led to new technologies being explored with, at times, some amazing results.

BREAKING ORBIT

Formed in Sydney around 2009 and quickly issued a couple of singles (*My direction* and *Callsign)* both in 2010, demonstrating their musical abilities with a heavy, melodic and atmospheric progressive sound.

'Firestarter' was the label for their debut album *The Time Traveller* (2012) and it is quite an amazing album and includes the two singles mentioned above.

The line-up for their debut was; *Matthew Quayle* (lead vocal/guitar), *Dylan Mitrovich* (guitar/percussion/ programming), *Ayden Mitrovich* (bass) and *Mark Tyson* (drums). *Dylan Mitrovich* also engineered, mixed and produced the album.

Echoes, is the opening track and showcases the melodic and atmospheric side without getting too heavy. Some soaring guitar lines are sublime and the drums captivating.

My Direction has some unique drumming and the use of, one assumes, some drum effects. Repeated (Eno Style) guitar is omnipresent and keyboards prominent. Certainly not a commercial sound and the reason it probably received little or no mainstream radio airplay. Heavy guitar is also in evidence but used sparingly.

Callsign was the other single and starts with heavy drums and guitar but once again was not overtly commercial. Some vocal borders on the metal growl without the intensity normally associated with the form.

The album has four instrumental tracks, three of which (*Machiguenga, Harmonic Voice* and *Ice Warmth*) feature a guest musician, *Amaru Ferrel* performing on bamboo flute or 'Quena' – a Peruvian instrument and one frequently used by buskers from an Inca background. All three tracks are glorious and atmospheric. The other instrumental, *Transcension (Pt 1)*, features some (almost classical sounding) guitar and is rather short but beautiful.

Orion is the heaviest track on the album with pounding drum and incessant rhythmic guitar lines.

Silence Seekers concludes a superb debut album with atmospheric effects and what sounds like clap-sticks. The mix of atmospherics, melody and heaviness is quite evident.

Sadly, my attempts to find their follow-up album on CD have proved fruitless. *Transcension* (2015) appears to continue along the same lines and contains two tracks following on from their debut, *Transcension pt 2* and *pt 3*. It is also not on a label and assumed independently released. Not available through the various websites I employ and not available on the band website I must resign myself to never owning it.

Equally annoying is the fact that no further information or releases can be found through my research. I hope it is just an extended hiatus and more will be forth-coming.

CLOSURE IN MOSCOW

Closure in Moscow, are a Melbourne band which formed in 2006. The line-up of *Christopher de Cinque* (vocals), *Mansur Zenneli* (guitar/vocals), *Michael Barrett* (guitar), *Brad Kimber* (bass) and *Beau McKee* (drums) performed on their first two releases.

Endeavouring to encapsulate their style in a few words proves somewhat difficult with the most over-blown description being 'a melodic blend of progressive avant-garde rock'. Perhaps the best comparison is *Mars Volta*.

I, personally have a preference for *Closure in Moscow* rather than *Mars Volta*. The band has some of the heaviness associated with progressive metal without fully embracing the genre. Vocals are often high register and a little difficult to decipher – thank goodness for printed lyrics.

The Penance and the Patience (2008) was released as an ep consisting of six tracks – the band called it an 'albumette'. Recorded at Melbourne's Sing Sing studios over several months it was produced and engineered by *Kris Crummett*.

It bears all the hallmarks of alternative/progressive rock and has a high-energy feel throughout. Initially released only in Australia and New Zealand and subsequently made available worldwide on digital download it achieved success by charting highly on the Australian Independent Record Album (ARIA) charts.

Their first full-length album was released in 2009 after the band had re-located to the United States in late 2008. Reconnecting with *Kris Crummett* for the recording and incorporating a variety of other instruments – including horns – the album displayed a greater diversity than their debut.

First Temple (2009) is a superior recording on all levels, containing twelve tracks detailing their composing and performing maturity – although they were all in their early twenties at the time – it achieved a higher position in the ARIA charts on release and nominated for an award under the 'hard rock/punk album' category. The mind boggles.

Sometime during 2010 *Kimber* and *McKee* were replaced by *Duncan Millar* and *Salvatore Aidone* respectively and the revamped line-up continues to date.

The first release by this incarnation of the band was *Pink Lemonade* (2014) and received mixed reviews and reactions from fans. Typical of those were some saying it was 'not what I expected' while others thought the new direction was very progressive. Some did comment on what they saw as 'mockery of the Christian faith and Jesus in particular' with tracks such as *The Church of the Technochrist*. It is for the individual to draw their own conclusion and as I have been unable to get a 'real' copy of the album I cannot comment. Tried various websites with only one available from the States and priced exorbitantly at around A$130 – I shall bide my time. On the band website the album has sold-out!

Meanwhile the band toured heavily in the UK and Europe gaining a growing fan-base although cancelled some shows after a series of misfortunes and anxiety over the Paris terror attacks. In 2016 they toured Australia for the first time in over eight years.

Writing for their third album got under way in 2017 but was postponed several times due to touring commitments, including sold-out concerts in Australia during their last tour down-under. As of the time of writing their website indicates that the album is under-going pre-production stating "it's been slow going" which is a consequence of repeated lockdowns.

I shall keep a sharp eye open for further developments as this is one band deserving of a wider audience.

EYEFEAR

Melbourne based progressive power metal band *Eyefear* came into existence in 1994 and are Australia's longest running metal band to date. It could have been so different but for the resilience of *Kosta (Con) Papazoglou*, *Rob Gorham* and *Zain Kimmie.*

With a mix of; power metal, progressive rock, melodic and symphonic sounds they sound like no other metal band I have come across and stand well alongside the likes of *Dream Theater* and *Fates Warning.*

Their early history through to the release of their second album witnessed, not only the aforesaid resilience but the coming and going of various band members just as things seemed settled. Their first album made great inroads and was hailed by many in prog and prog metal circles as a debut exhibiting superb musicianship and outstanding lyrics – with just the right amount of 'dark matter'. It was not too long after that release that many thought, with all the upheavals, the end of the band was a foregone conclusion. The full details are not within the parameters of these short stories but can be easily accessed through websites and I would personally recommend *spirit-of-metal.com.*

Edge of Existence (1996) was recorded from late 1995 through to early 1996 and catapulted the band into the consciousness of prog and metal fans around the world garnering favourable reviews.

My copy is priceless – for me anyway – as it has *Zain Kimmie's* autograph on the cover. The music matured in time and this album exhibits a more hard rock edge than metal. Top track is *The Running Man* but the whole album is excellent and well worth adding to any collection – a little difficult to track down these days.

The future looked bright indeed but then...they appeared to vanish.

Dawn A New Beginning (1999), a three track ep was titled ambitiously and prematurely as it proved anything but. Of the three tracks two would appear on their next full-length album. For now, though, it looked extremely unlikely that that would happen.

Enter keyboardist *Garrett Ryan* and vocalist *Danny Cecati* (the latter from Australian metal band *Pagazus*) and optimism rises once more only to be dashed again when *Ryan* left then came back only to leave again. *Cecate* on the other hand played a quite incredible role in the future of *Eyefear. Ryan's* replacement was *Sammy Giaccotto* prior to the release of their next album which was in the recording process at the time. The line-up for which was; *Danny Cecati* (vocals), *Kosta Papazoglou* (guitar), *Rob Gorham* (bass), *Sammy Giaccotto* (keyboards) and *Zain Kimmie* (drums).

9 Elements of Inner Vision (2004) is a remarkable album given the background and struggle to hold a cohesive line-up together. The two tracks from the *Dawn ep* trans-ferred to the album blended in very well with the newer material and both *Dawn* and *Illumination Fades* are excel-lent tracks on an excellent album. Picking out a personal highlight is quite difficult but the mini-epic '*While the world sleeps pt 1 Dreams* and *pt 2 Altered Visions*' are worth pulling out the album for.

A bonus DVD was included with the band in live perfor-mance and a video clip of *Two souls apart.*

Many, mistakenly but understandably, viewed this as their debut album given the amazing eight year gap.

Onward and upward was the only way to go from here and this time that resilience and optimism paid off.

A World full of grey (2007) with the same stable line-up enhanced their profile immensely and it was their best to date remaining a firm favourite among fans old and new.

The opening is quite operatic with drums and keyboards highly prominent but it is the vocals which tear strips off the flesh. The high register gives way to a more subtle approach as *Danny Cecati* 'underscores' his importance to the overall sound.

The title track follows and is a more subdued metal assault – without that sounding like a contradiction.

A trend which began on the previous album continues with another two part epic of *'While the world sleeps'*. Once again it is difficult not to see these as absolute stand-outs. It is worth combining all four parts should you have the equipment to do so.

I cannot praise this album too much with its changing tempo, complexity and subtleness often lacking with other metal bands. The vocals, at times, sound reminiscent of *Ian Gillan* (circa *Child in Time*) and a symphonic feel often raises its head to great effect.

Bassist and founding member *Rob Gorham* left the band during 2008 and bass parts on their next album were performed by *Kosta*. Another bassist would take some time to find.

The Unseen (2008) is an altogether heavier album than its predecessor but still maintains the ingredients of; melody, atmosphere and lyrical brilliance. A progression for sure but a feeling of 'marking time' is never too far off.

The Unseen is the real standout from this set with keyboards dominating while the vocals are powerful and strong. The 'chugging' guitar is affective but the bass is well down in the mix – perhaps *Kosta* wasn't that pleased with his playing, who can say.

From darkness till dawn has an early *Dream Theater* feel to it without going totally in that direction. It may well be the vocals as both vocalists have the capacity to hit those high notes with apparent ease.

Overall though, this is not the first choice album pulled from the shelf when I play some *Eyefear*.

Rob Gorham's eventual replacement was *Evan Harris* but another change was looming. Soon *Sammy Giaccotto* departed and was replaced by *Seb Schneider.* Together with; *Kosta, Danny* and *Zain* they would repair to make their next album.

If *The Unseen* was 'marking time' the next album proved a full-ahead rush into uncharted waters.

The Inception of Darkness (2012) proved to be their last studio album to date but what an album it is.

Lyrically this is a gargantuan leap forward and compliments both music and vocals with keyboards and drums being the most dominant instruments.

Eyes of Madness contains vocals which reflect the title sounding somewhat manic at times.

Again – I'm sucker for them – the mini-epic is superb. It is the title track in two parts, *Transcending* and *Reborn* respectively. They segue beautifully and represent the absolute high point of the album. There is a little metal growl from guest vocalist *George Kosmas*, which I don't mind if it is not over done.

Seb Schneider was replaced by *Rueben Stone* but repeated searches have revealed nothing in the way of new material forth-coming and the last news of any note was that as of 2019 *Danny Cecati* will be fronting 'fist pumping hard rockers' *Wicked Smile.*

Whether this is the end for *Eyefear* has not been confirmed one way or the other. Perhaps it is an extended hiatus which has been extended further by the global pandemic.

This great Australian band can possibly rise again and display that resilience for which they became renowned.

PLINI

Plini Roessler-Holgate records and tours simply as *Plini.*

Born in Sydney in 1992 his style is described variously as; instrumental rock, progressive rock, post-rock and jazz fusion. He began his career when just 19 years old and recently released his second full-length album.

His main instrument is guitar and he has been called a 'prodigy' while his albums list the various musicians appearing then state that *Plini* performs 'everything else'.

His main source of inspiration and influence comes from none other than *Joe Satriani* and *Steve Vai* and those influences do indeed come through at times. His unique instrumental music covers several genres with blues and jazz taking centre stage.

Most artists would be outraged when someone blatantly uses their music but *Plini* recently took it in his very casual stride when America rapper *Doja Cat's* hit *Say So* appeared to plagiarise music from his album *Handmade Cities* (2016). His response was more laid-back than many of his fans who took to forums to vent their anger. *Plini* however saw it as great advertising and seemed mildly amused by all the fuss.

His music is available through his website and the same casual and very hands-on approach comes to the fore when

I purchased his latest album with a personal 'thank you' and letting me know it was on its way.

He had three eps to his credit prior to releasing his first album; *Other Things* (2013), *Sweet Nothings* (2013) and *The end of Everything* (2015) all display a virtuoso guitarist – and everything else!

Handmade Cities (2016) was to draw praise, not just from prog fans but also from some of his peers with comments by *Steve Vai* in particular effusive in his praise for the album. He described it as melodic and harmonically deep before declaring it the "finest guitar record he had ever heard"

He does exhibit modesty when people praise his music and liken him to some of his (obvious) hero's which is refreshing indeed.

Sunhead (2018) is a four track ep released independently which *Plini* composed, arranged and produced. It draws on several styles and for me personally I find the jazz fusion so pleasing without being cliché.

Simon Grove (bass) and *John Waugh* (saxophone) are just two of the talented musicians with whom he records and I'm reminded of *Steve Hackett* with his approach in bringing superb musicians on-board without hogging the limelight.

Impulse Voices (2000) continues in a similar vein and has become a 'high rotation' album for me.

I'll tell you something has a harder-edged sound and is even more welcome for that. This is when some heard *Satriani* influences peeking through – an observation *Plini* is "cool" with.

The title track is also glorious and the final track *The glass bead game* rounds out this wonderful album with a contribution on harp by *Amy Turk*.

Plini, like every other musician world-wide has been impacted by the on-going pandemic which has brought no end of problems and suffering but like all others he too welcomes the opportunity to get back doing what he does best rather than quarantining and isolating.

Perhaps then he will reach the wider audience of which his music is very much deserving.

SEBASTIAN HARDIE

The first time I have travelled back to the seventies as, sadly, I feel Australia's contributions at the time fell short of the excellent bands in the UK, Europe and the US. They lacked the fullness and grandeur which northern hemisphere audiences grew accustomed to. I may be doing some an injustice but little of what I have experienced since arriving in Australia has made a lasting impact – good though some of it undoubtedly was.

Sebastian Hardie first appeared on the Australian scene in 1967 as *Sebastian Hardie Blues Band* playing rhythm and blues and soul covers but soon dropped the *Blues Band* playing a more pop-oriented style. Basically remaining a covers band they performed songs be the likes of, the *Rolling Stones, the Beatles* and other pop luminaries of the time. The ever revolving line-ups saw some members go on to greater success with other Australian bands, such as *Dennis Laughlin* who joined *Sherbet* as their vocalist and *Jon English* who latterly performed theatre, in particular the popular *Pirates of Penzance.* It was not until 1973 that the progressive rock style was introduced and remains the genre for which they are best known.

The line-up by 1973 was; *Mario Milo* – sometimes spelt as *Millo* – (vocal/lead guitar), *Steve Dunn* (keyboards), *Peter Plavsic* (bass) and *Alex Plavsic* (drums and percussion). *Dunn* was replaced by *Toivo Pilt* in 1974 and both bass and drum saw a revolving door policy as the line-up gelled mainly in and around *Mario Milo.*

They have gone down in history as Australia's first symphonic rock band with a style not dissimilar of *YES* without the alternating dynamics for which *YES* became renowned during their earliest period.

Four Moments (1975) was produced by ex-member *Jon English* and achieved 'gold' status in Australia being compared to; *Genesis, Yes, King Crimson* and *Focus* – all of whom were at their absolute peak at the time.

It contained lengthy and complex instrumental passages with the bulk of the lyrical content appearing of *Glories shall be released.* It was impeccable musicianship married to amazing arrangements and flowing progressive symphonic music.

Windchase (1976) did not receive the plaudits or success of their debut and even though the track *Life, Love and Music* was released as a single it too failed to make an impact.

The overall feel of the album varies little from their debut and some found the long and intricate instrumental sections, well, boring. Equally they were still performing as a support act and during 1976 supported *Santana* on their Australian tour.

Internal strife and management problems took their inevitable toll and they disbanded with *Milo* and *Pilt* performing under the name *Windchase.*

Windchase played material written by *Milo* then released the album *Symphinity* (1977) which bordered on jazz fusion. The arrival of 'punk' and 'new wave', offering an alternative to prog, made an impact on *Windchase* and they too disbanded.

Variations of the band under differing names and line-ups performed over the years before a full-blown reunion – albeit brief – in 1994.

Four moments of the windchase (1990) was released by *Startrax* and gathers over 60 minutes of music from their two albums. Superbly compiled for a low-budget release it remains available while their original albums are hard to track down.

The 1994 reunion saw them perform ProgFest in Los Angeles which was recorded and released three years later as *Sebastian Hardie – Live in L.A.* (1997). Combining *Four Moments, Windchase, Symphinity* and *Epic III* (the latter a solo album by *Mario Milo* released in 1979) it is a wonderful document of a band which never achieved their potential but retained a devoted fan base in Australia.

A second reunion occurred in 2003, which as of the time of writing still appears to be on-going, in support of *Yes* during their Australian tour. I was able to attend this concert and *Sebastian Hardie* performed an incredible set which was marred by an over-zealous roadie and *Steve Howe's* guitar tech. He thought the band was over-staying their welcome as support and promptly 'pulled the plug'. Roundly booed by the Melbourne audience the 'karma bus' visited this roadie and *Howe* could be seen ripping into him as no end of technical problems irked the guitarist. One just hopes *Yes* were unaware and duly offered *Sebastian*

Hardie (who considered supporting them a privilege) a deserved apology.

Blueprint (2011) proved their first new material and was received warmly by long-time fans with one commenting in his review "write a masterpiece, skip forward 37 years, write another".

It followed the tried and trusted formula and perhaps for some was too dated and offered nothing new but to many it was welcomed with open arms.

The last activity of any note was a live performance by *Mario Milo* from 2018 and released as *Performs Four Moments (Live in Tokyo)*.

Perhaps that is where things will remain but various links still have them listed as 'active'.

They certainly activated my interest and remain the true pioneers of Australian prog.

TERAMAZE

Geelong is Victoria's second largest city and is situated some 70 km (45ml) from Melbourne. Over the years it has been synonymous with the Ford Motor Company, employer to many in the population. It also boasts one of the Australian Football League's (Aussie Rules) oldest and most successful clubs. Tourists will also find it the 'Gateway' to many attractions – the most renowned and popular being the Great Ocean Road scenic drive.

Nightlife is vibrant with a live music scene to rival many cities of similar size and in fact has produced some of Australia best known celebrities such as; Barry Crocker, Jeff Lang and Chrissy Amphlett. Music festivals also thrive (in pandemic free times) and include the Queenscliff Music Festival.

Geelong is less known for being the home of one of Australia's premier progressive metal bands, *Teramaze,* who likely played many of the cities venues and gained a reputation for their early 'thrash' metal style.

Terrormaze had their beginnings around 1993 and are still active in 2021 – issuing new music, now under the name *Teramaze.* The name change was the result of embracing Christianity which also saw the 'thrash' style moderated and lyrical themes reflecting their choice of life-style without being 'preachy'.

Dean Wells (guitar and vocals) has been present for almost the entire life-span of the band and the only founding member in the current line-up.

Their early material did not draw me in with the emphasis definitely 'thrash' power metal and the first two full-length studio albums – *Doxology* (1995) and *Tears to Dust* (1998) – never found favour.

They also issued an ep *Not the Criminal* (2001) and another album, albeit a collection of earlier material *Anthology* (2006)

It was not until the release of *Anhedonia* (2012) that I began taking notice as the transition from 'thrash' to a more melodic, although still power metal, style emerged.

Esoteric Symbolism (2014) proved the album to draw me in. By this time the band had gone through several line-up changes including the death of one *Julian Percy* (drums). He can be heard on the *Anhedonia* album and was a very powerful force.

The line-up for the 2014 album proved to be; *Dean Wells* (guitar, bass, vocals and keyboards), *Brett Rerekura* (vocals),

John Zambelis (guitar) and *Dean Kennedy* (drums). It was an album which would complete the transition from overtly 'thrash metal'.

Esoteric Symbolism remains powerful but has a sound not dissimilar to *Dream Theater* or *Tool* without emulating either. The dynamics range from power metal to intricately melodic moments with a driving vocal, heavy drumming and some virtuosic guitar soloing. This was the way forward as subsequent albums attest.

'*All seeing Eye*' opens proceedings with an instrumental which begins quietly and builds until the metal assault kicks in through to the end. From here it just gets better and a great way for those unfamiliar with the band to discover their sound.

'*Darkest days of Symphony*' is a firm favourite of mine with a beautifully delivered introduction displaying a vocal range which is appealing. The track builds slowly but powerfully until some superb guitar breaks in. The vocal returns and slows things down a little before picking up and concluding with drums and vocal almost contesting one another.

By the time their next album appeared the line-up had undergone some changes with *Nathan Peachy* replacing *Brett Rerekura* on vocals and *Luis Eguren* (bass) joining the band at the expense of *John Zambelis* (guitar). This left *Dean Wells* as the single guitarist and relieved him of bass duties. *Dave Holley* (keyboards and sound effect) is credited but listed separately from the rest of the band.

Her Halo (2015) has been cited by many as not just their best album up to the time of its release but the best overall. I have difficulty not agreeing as the progression is there for all to hear. It is one played often and one which is timeless in its appeal.

'*An Ordinary Dream*' is the opening track and an epic which underscores the great advances made in just one year between albums.

'*Delusions of Grandeur*' closes the album with another epic and both tracks book-end this concept of two sisters wonderfully.

The atmospherics and power are complimentary and the harmonising between *Peachy* and *Wells* is majestic. The keyboards add a dimension which was hitherto unexplored. The guitar soloing remains of a standard worthy of *John Petrucci (Dream Theater)* – one of *Well's* cited influences.

Undoubted commitments such as touring in support of *Her Halo* meant a four year gap ensued before the next release. During that time considerable line-up changes took place.

Dean Wells is in place but *Brett Rerekura* returns as vocalist. *Andrew Cameron* (bass), *Jonah Weingarten* (keyboards), *Chris Zoupa* (guitar) and *Rob Brens* (drums) were all recent additions, but *Rob Brens* was soon replaced by *Nick Ross*. As of 2021 the line-up is now a four-piece consisting of; *Dean Wells, Chris Zoupa, Andrew Cameron* and *Nick Ross*.

'*Are We Soldiers*' (2019) continues the progression and the six-member band stretch and extend their signature sound remarkably.

I reviewed this album on a couple of forums referring to it as 'another Aussie gem' and noting that my attention was drawn to the band through a UK magazine. I also noted that yet another "Aussie band flies under the highly commercial world of radio and television in their own backyard" It was my considered opinion at the time and I see no reason to alter that opinion.

The band has been busy over the last 18 months releasing two albums during a period which has witnessed our world turned upside-down with the global pandemic coronavirus (covid-19).

I Wonder (2020) was extremely well received by the metal and prog communities and comments such as "a contender for Album of the Year" rating it 10/10 for; song-writing, musicianship, memorability and production are common place. What does one add, other than be in total agreement with the reviewer.

Sorella Minore (2021) is the second instalment of *Her Halo.* It is a continuation of the concept and tumultuous story of two sisters.

I have yet to hear this album but it is on order. The opening track is an incredible 26 minute epic followed by three tracks of 'shorter duration'.

What makes the epic so different is the inclusion of four vocalist of outstanding quality – all Australian. *Nathan Peachy* makes a welcome return to the fold and his harmonising with *Dean Wells* has been considered previously. The other two are; *Silvio Massaro (Vanishing Point)* and *Jennifer Borg (Divine Ascension).*

The website announcement concludes with the statement "Prepare to experience *Teramaze* like you never have before".

I look forward to doing so.

This is more by way of a postscript. While waiting for *Sorella Minore* to arrive I jumped on their website and ordered *I Wonder* as I did not have a physical copy.

To my utter surprise, a few days later, around 6.30 pm as we sat watching the evening news I received a phone call but couldn't completely grasp what was being said (thought it may have been a tele-marketer). I asked for clarification, and I am convinced he said it was *Nick Ross* and that he had just slipped my two CDs into our mailbox – he does live close by. Thanking him he returned the thanks for the order and support. I rushed out to the mailbox but not a soul was in sight but there were my two CDs. What a fantastic lockdown surprise!

The following morning I sent a message to the number and wished all associated with *Teramaze* well. The reply was "Hahaha all good man! Thanks so much for the support".

Sorella Minore is everything I expected and more. What an amazing album the guys have come up with. I'm calling it an album even though it is advertised as an ep. Around 40 minutes duration over the four tracks I'm happy with 'album'.

The epic opening track far surpasses expectations but I haven't had sufficient listens to pen a full review – which will be extremely favourable.

Thank you to all involved with *Teramaze,* you have made this fan one happy man and displayed the kind of attention to detail which permeates the prog community.

Latest news is pre-ordering is up and running for their new album '*And the beauty they perceive*'.

THE THIRD ENDING

Hailing from Hobart, Tasmania – that island off the south-eastern coast of Australia which often gets left off maps of Australia – *The Third Ending* formed back in 2002 by *Andrew Curtis* (guitar), *Nick Storr* (vocal, guitar and keyboards), *Cornel Ianculovici* (bass) and *Andrew Knott* (drums and percussion) and presented a style of progressive rock all their own. Some saw it as 'crossover-prog'.

Incorporating rock and metal they also display melodic acoustic and neo-prog elements to form a melting pot of influences and have been likened to; *Dream Theater, Pink Floyd, Porcupine Tree* and *Spock's Beard*. Personally I find more of a *Cryptic Vision* sound coming through but comparisons can be tiresome although they help the uninitiated to get some idea of a band's style.

The first two years saw the band feverishly working on their debut album which was released twice, once independently and again by their record company Prog Rock Records.

The Third Ending (2007) drew high praise from some in Melbourne's prog community with local guitarist *Michael Mills* effusively proclaiming them "the finest Australian progressive rock band ever".

I will not get so carried away although their debut album is superb on every level – musicianship, song-writing, powerful when needed subtle when not and exuding fluidity.

Hard to pick just one song as a total stand-out so I have chosen two because they segue beautifully.

Part V and *Coming Around* end the album although there is a reprise of an earlier song *Fingerprints* which closes the album totally. These two songs present a smorgasbord of prog influences and styles but do not become cliché. At times it is possible to hear all the influences and comparisons that many have noted but again I will say they have stamped their own personalities all over these songs.

To look at the other side of the coin some forums were less enthusiastic in their praise than *Michael Mills*. Generally the star rating hovered between 3 and 3.5 with some feeling that given time and backing the band would be a force. That seems a bit harsh to me but everyone is entitled to their own opinion.

Not a prolific band by any means it proved a full seven years prior to a follow-up release leaving many to believe they had 'done their dash'.

Three Word Title (2014) received better reviews in general but was still struggling to reach 4 star ratings even though some saw it is a an accessible and melodic slice of modern progressive rock. Others thought the track '*Bullet in winter*' had a sound reminiscent of *Marillion* – I do not and do not believe they set out to sound like anybody else in spite of their influences.

Sadly nothing else has been forth-coming and my endeavours to contact the band have been fruitless and the website has an abandoned look with the last up-date around their second album release.

Nonetheless these are worth seeking out for any serious prog collector or just for the curious.

VOYAGER

Daniel Estrin, Mark Barker and *Adam Lovkis* had attended the University of Western Australia in Perth when they decided to form the progressive metal band *Voyager* in 1999. The only one from the trio still with the band is *Estrin* with the other founding members departing very quickly.

The arrivals and departures continued for the next decade before a more stable line-up gelled and today the band consists of; *Danny (Daniel) Estrin* (lead vocal and keyboards), *Simone Dow* (guitar), *Alex Canion* (bass), *Scott Kay* (guitar) and *Ashley Doodkorte* (drums).

Element V (2003) was released to great acclaim and saw the band tour extensively in its support including a European tour which raised their profile and ensured a rapidly growing following.

One reviewer of the album remarked the band "seemed to come out of nowhere". This of course ignores all the hard work to get to this stage and reminded one of an 'overnight sensation' in 1963, *the Beatles,* who had done the hard yards treading the boards for some six years before breaking through!

The album sets out their stall with strong song structures, virtuoso playing and atmospheric moments incorporating melody. This remains their modus operandi to this day.

Europe provided a platform to perform for 'prog' audiences at venues, particularly in the Netherlands, suited for the genre and brought them to the attention of the German record label Dockyard 1 through which their next album saw release.

uniVers (2007) received a world-wide release and brought them to the attention of American audiences with several magazines and websites extolling the album and band. Their star was also on the rise back in Australia with radio and other media attention.

Shortly after another line-up shuffle occurred with *Melissa Fiocco* replaced by *Alex Canion* on bass – a position he currently retains. During his first tour of Australia they toured with *Eyefear* on what has been described as a mini-tour.

The survival of any artist(s) is more dependent on the record buying public and their music was receiving plaudits from prog/metal fans and, more importantly, selling well.

A planned tour of the UK in 2008 had to be cancelled due to poor sales but they toured mainland Europe with some success. Then guitarist *Mark De Vattimo* decided to quit citing 'personal and musical differences'.

I am the reVolution (2009) witnessed perhaps, the first negative criticism with some feeling strong melodies reflected a 'pop' sound not in vogue within prog/metal circles generally. Personally it is this very element which drew me to them and long may it continue.

In 2010 *Scott Kay* replaced the departing *Chris Hanssen* on guitar and immediately set off on tour, a tour which brought them critical acclaim.

A new decade and a new label – with America's 'Sensory' – was followed by the release of a new album.

The Meaning of I (2011) was the first with *Scott Kay* but the last with drummer *Mark Boeijen*. It features guest vocalists and in particular *Daniel Tompkins (TesseracT)*. Released in America earlier than elsewhere due to their appearance at the ProgPower festival it nonetheless enhanced their position and garnered more critical acclaim.

Crowd funding is nothing new to many of the world's progressive rock bands with *Marillion* at the forefront, in 2013 *Voyager* ventured down this path putting a very successful campaign together for their projected album *V* which was released following year.

Meanwhile they continued touring relentlessly and supporting many big names, mainly in Europe and America.

V (2014) probably gained negative and positive response in equal measure but this is an album brimming with all the elements which *Voyager* have in their arsenal. *Breaking Down* and *Hyperventilating* are the epitome of all they stand for and they alone make this an album worth having. *Seasons of Age* end the album superbly with heavy bass and drum and a wonderful chorus.

Ghost Mile (2017) proved my first purchase as I had previously been only vaguely aware of the band. It remains my favourite album because it formed the doorway to their amazing mix of melodic progressive metal with an AOR feel.

Ascension is a fantastic opening track and is followed by *Misery is only Company*. Both come close for my choice of best on album but for the absolutely superb closing track 'As the city takes the Night'.

2018 saw the band perform at O2 Indigo, London during the European Space Agency's exhibition. They performed two songs from the forth-coming and seventh full-length studio album *Colours* and *Brightstar*.

'Colours in the Sun' (2019) is described by the website as, well, "colourful". Certainly the CD cover art is very colourful but what of the music? The website describes *Voyager* as a "pop/prog/power/rock/metal force" – just about covers everything.

Verbosity is something I am generally not accused of so I will endeavour to keep this brief but may exhaust all superlatives along the way.

Simply, *Colours in the Sun* is a superb album and embraces all the converging genres listed on their website. It embraces a more 'pop/prog' direction without sacrificing the metal element but with a more melodic style and vocals (sometimes harmonising) to compliment the music.

The ten tracks are all relatively short by progressive rock standards but each deserves repeated listens.

Saccharine Dream is my personal pick for best on album and is anything but saccharine with some excellent lead guitar.

Water over the Bridge is another brilliant track and encompasses all the genres described above from their website.

Runaway ends the album in superb fashion and could – should they have decided to – made a great single.

This is a direction which keeps *Voyager* progressing and one it is hoped they continue with.

Voyager are another amazing Australian band that keep the progressive flag flying and bringing great music to fans at home and abroad.

in CONCLUSION

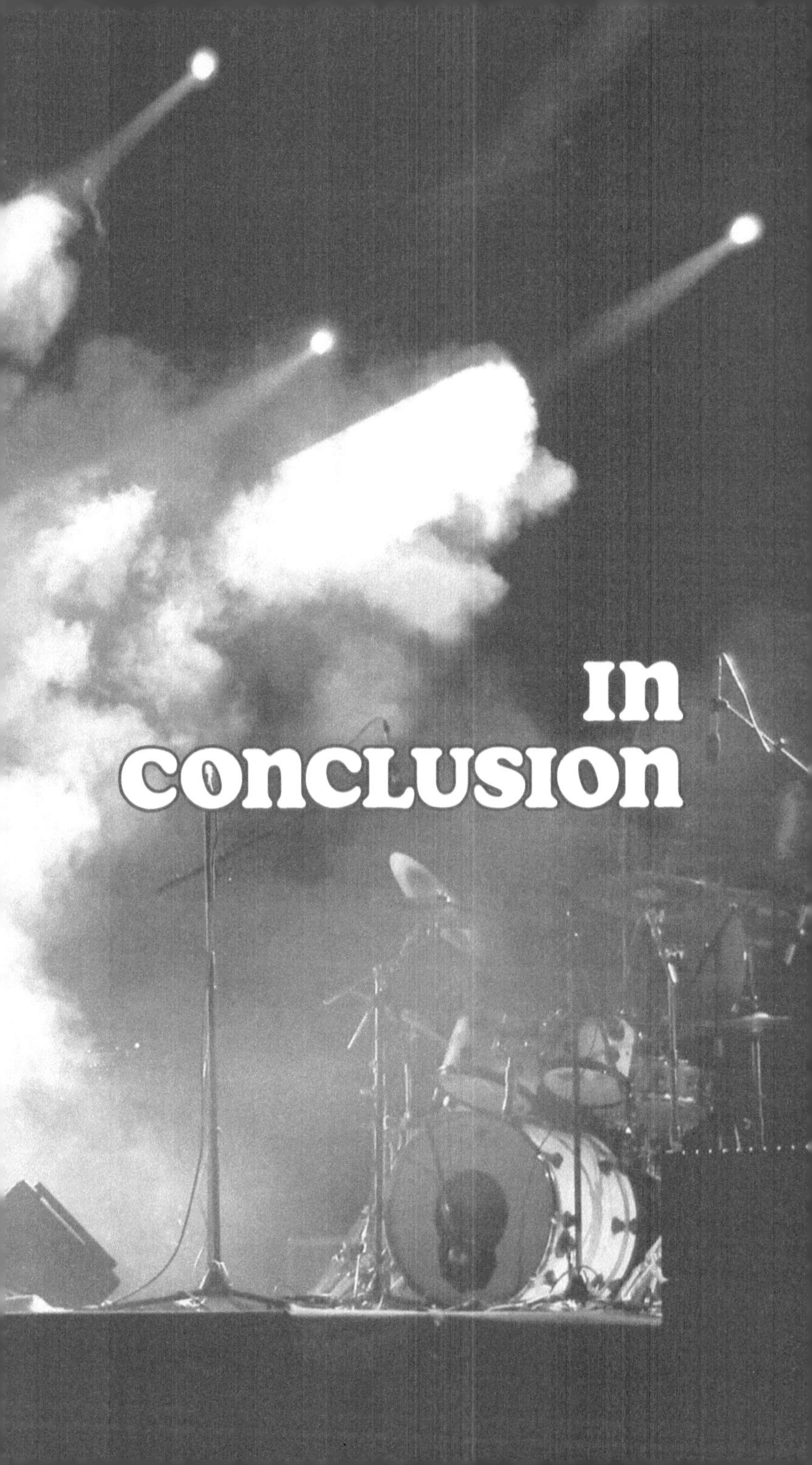

IT IS NOW LATE August 2021 and in the state of Victoria, Australia we are experiencing our sixth lock-down with little hope of coming out of it this side of Christmas. The restrictions imposed are the toughest experienced and include the closure of; all hospitality, all venues, playgrounds and skateboard parks, travel limits of immediate area only and childcare centres. Mask to be worn except at home. No visitors, funeral and wedding limits of ten. As we say in Victoria "the worst part of a seven day lock-down is the third week!"

The havoc wrought by this pandemic touches everyone's lives and the subjects of this book have had to put plans to tour and even record on hold. The financial impact may result in some never performing live again but a small ray of hope appeared in this morning's newspaper. A campaign under the banner 'Please don't stop the Music' has been launched here in Victoria to ensure; musicians, bands and venues will have their bills paid for cancelled gigs during the lock-downs. Its hope is to keep the struggling industry alive. The industry as a whole employs so many people who have been unable to work for the last eighteen months as crowds at venues and outdoor concerts have been considered too high a risk.

Without exception the artists (remotely) interviewed declared their intension to get back out 'on the road' as soon as circumstances allow and get back in touch with their audiences – that is good news.

On a personal level certain events have had to be curtailed or postponed. My wife Louise has had to cancel a planned trip to Western Australia three times and eventually re-scheduled for next year. We both had plans to be in Ireland for my Dad's 95th but had to make do with a phone call.

Sadly my first wife died recently but we all managed to attend a 'proper' funeral with some coming over the border from South Australia. Afterward, while we sat around talking, a lock-down was announced to start from mid-night. All those from other states had to depart very quickly to avoid quarantine and being caught in Victoria for an indefinite period – a sad end to a very sad day.

When I set out to write this book it was prior to the launch of my first 'Progressive Rock Unmasked'. That experience taught me many things and I thank my proof-reader Lynne Carmichael for some excellent tuition. I believe my writing skills have improved as a result.

The other thing I decided to do (once I had short-listed the subjects) was to contact as many as possible for inclusion. Their comments, time and encouragement have meant a great deal to me and I whole-heartedly offer my sincerest thanks to them all. I feel it added to the stories and being able to meet with some was a wonderful bonus. They proved the prog community is tight-knit and welcoming.

Obviously the artists included in no way covers the great depth and number of fine musicians Australia has flying under the 'prog' banner but was intended to be an introduction with the hope that you, the reader, may take it on yourself to research and support our growing progressive rock scene.

The uncertain times we are living in mean many are unable to tour and bring their music to us. We can, though, financially help support them in their endeavours to keep making the music we all enjoy. Jump on their websites and purchase the merchandise and music – in whatever form suits you. Hopefully live music will soon make a welcome return and we can enjoy together watching and listening to our great performers.

During a brief period of 'freedom' I was able to watch and listen as the band *Malcura* ran through their paces at a local venue and wish to express my thanks to the band for inviting me along. I had a wonderful time and will not forget their kindness.

The future of progressive music in Australia looks assured and judging by the responses of the interviewees they will continue to bring us 'great art'. Equally and also assuredly, new bands and artist will appear on the horizon and continue the progression – that is what we all want.

It is my earnest hope that you have enjoyed reading 'Prog Rock Down-under' with my thoughts and experiences of the artists considered. I have been at pains to point out that the views and opinions expressed are personally held and in no way intended to cause offense or to sway any from listening and enjoying the music presented by those artists.

For well over 50 years I have been enjoying progressive music in one form or another. The palette is full and the various artists offer their musical ideas on a wide and colourful canvas. I don't buy into the idea that a certain type of music in not prog because it doesn't sound like 'so-and-so'. Progression means advancing ideas and styles and should never be limited to one style. We, like the artists, need to be adventurous and develop a more catholic taste. Taking time out to give all 'a fair go' will encourage the musicians to produce music which continues to progress and keep the genre alive.

Some of my friends and acquaintances – when they discovered I was writing about prog – asked me to define progressive rock. Just what it is that makes it so different from other musical forms?

My stock answer was that it is music which challenges the listener and embraces many genres. It does break the rules but as one high profile artist once observed "you've got to know the rules to break them".

The other thing which I felt needed further explanation was the differing opinions held by many regarding just what prog is, or isn't.

Over the years many have voiced their opinions – as they are entitled to do – but decry a band for their latest offering as it veers away from the genre or it doesn't adhere to their idea of progressive music. Some seem to feel that any change with the structure or line-up borders on the 'unforgivable sin'. The English progressive rock band '*YES*' have been active since the late sixties and, not surprisingly, have had a succession of musicians come and go – sadly that includes the death of founding member and mainstay *Chris Squire*. *YES* forums are inundated with fans objecting to one thing or another – usually a change in the line-up. Their albums are dissected and opined on to such a degree one wonders if they actually enjoy them! I have previously said that *YES* fans are the most fickle fans I know. Nothing I read will change that opinion. Their last studio album was lambasted by some with one in particular advising readers not to buy as this is not *YES* in any way, shape of form. It is actually not a bad album.

Another artist is *Steven Wilson*. *Wilson* has had many 'projects' over the years with (arguably) his best loved being *Porcupine Tree*. He has offered up a veritable smorgasbord of music but nonetheless was berated for more recent work because many failed to see it as progressive. This is where I take exception with those opinions. Surely progressive means moving on, not adhering to a tried and tested formula but stretching out and adventurously expressing new ideas.

YES and *Steven Wilson* are of course not Australian but English nonetheless the same lamentable attacks have been levelled at some of Australia's finest and possibly prevented them from exploring a certain direction for fear of alienating the fan-base. Some press on regardless and for me that is to be praised and encouraged.

In conclusion I thank you for purchasing my 'little' book and thank the Australian artists who have provided me with such great entertainment over the years. Being a professed fan of the genre often leads some to remark that it is not music you can dance to or music which gets played on the radio. They seem to believe it is not a popular form of music. "Well" I encourage "go on any search engine and type in 'progressive rock' to see how many websites come up and attest to its popularity".

Long may that continue and long may musicians the world over continue to explore new avenues of expression that 'true progressive rock fans' can enjoy.

AFTER-THOUGHTS

DUE TO UNFORESEEN CIRCUMSTANCES I had to postpone the publication of this book by several months – close to a year in fact.

During the previous year or so my family has dealt with (and is still dealing with) the death of three very loved and cherished members.

Firstly, my first wife Elayne – mother of our three children – died after a protracted battle with cancer. This is dealt with in the body of this book, but the aftereffects continue and will continue for some time to come.

Just before the end of 2021 a much-loved uncle – Sammy Logue – died suddenly while in care due to the onset of dementia. He was a larger-than-life character who exuded love for family and friends.

Sadly, my dad died in February 2022 and due to the pandemic restrictions, we were unable to travel safely to Ireland for his funeral. That made coping and accepting harder on myself and family living far away.

Dad was brought up during the depression and catastrophic second world war – this shaped his attitude on many things. In retrospect he always made sure his family was cared for and catered for, taking his responsibilities seriously. He cared for mum, who died ten years previously.

I try not to dwell on the thought of making a return to Ireland and he is no longer there. He lived a long and dignified life and fulfilled his motto of "living long enough to be the best version of himself that he possibly could".

We also had two very close and dear friends die this last year and another suffering the effects of cancer as I write.

In addition to the human tragedies, we lost our two beautiful King Charles Cavaliers within months of one another. Sally (10) with serious heart problems and Noah (15 ½) from old age.

All-in-all not conducive to compiling a book, however short!

For every yin there is a yang and the delay resulted in being able to add the *Anubis* reissue of their debut album *230503* (2002). It is superb with the bonus disc offering a new rendition of the track '*The Life not Taken*' in its totality for the first time. Grateful thanks to *David Eaton* for passing on his and the bands condolences.

Another amazing event happened in late 2021 – the reformation of *Unitopia*. I responded to a post on Facebook regarding the album *Artificial* noting that even though *Unitopia* was no longer people should check out *Southern Empire* or *United Progressive Fraternity*.

Within a short space of time *Mark Trueack* posted the news (to me anyway) that they had reformed with two new members – *Chester Thompson* and *Alphonso Johnson* – and a new album in progress *Seven Chambers* (2022). Sorry Mark, I was otherwise preoccupied!

Besides this they are working on another (yet unnamed) album.

The live scene is also starting to raise its head again and my twice postponed *Steve Hackett Genesis Revisited* concert will be performed on the 23rd of June 2022.

A positive note on which to conclude after all the heartache endured these past twelve months.

PROG ON and "don't live for today like you were immortal". Cheers – Colin Logue

50 Influential Albums

The criteria had to be simple, these albums had to reflect those that made a huge impact personally but choosing just 50 from the thousands I have listened to over the years and from a collection of over 1400 was extremely difficult and I spent more time in selection than writing.

The final choices were difficult and omitted many albums more than worthy of inclusion, including *The Beatles Revolver* (1966) and *Abbey Road* (1969) – both progressive in their day.

It is not intended to present these albums as a 'countdown', elevating one over the other, but alphabetically – when more than one entry appears for an artist they will appear chronologically.

Progressive rock has always been a genre of extremes in style from the power metal to the experimental and ambient, symphonic to jazz infused and beyond. Equally the albums run the gauntlet from conceptually based to stand-alone songs.

It is hoped that most of this will be covered in my choices from over fifty years of listening to progressive music.

Whatever your viewpoint of the finished list it is worth remembering that it represents 50 albums only and many great albums will not have made my personal list. Culling down was a difficult task and every endeavor was made to offer an eclectic selection which hopefully will sway readers to delve into areas they hitherto have not ventured.

Anubis – A Tower of Silence (2011)

Anubis hale from Sydney, Australia and present progressive rock which is cinematically symphonic and expansive along with thought provoking lyrics.

Robert James Moulding (vocals/percussion/guitar) and *David Eaton* (keyboards/guitar) were the founding members and the line-up changed from time to time. On this album they were joined by *Douglas Skene* (Guitar), *Dean Bennison* (guitar/clarinet), *Steven Eaton* (drums/percussion) and *Nicholas Antoinette* (bass). It is also notable that all contribute vocals, and the harmonies shine through on this album.

A Tower of Silence proved the follow-up to their immensely well received debut *230503* (2008) clearly highlighting a band with talent to burn and brimming with virtuosic musicianship.

The opening epic *The Passing Bell (Part I–VI)* displays all of the above mentioned in full measure as well as setting the scene for the album as a whole.

Conceptually a ghost story in the classic sense regarding an 11-year-old girl who worked and died in a Victorian workhouse in England and found her 'spirit' trapped in the building. Some years pass and a group of girls enter the, now abandoned, building and decide to conduct a séance. They inadvertently raise her trapped spirit and her story unfolds through a superb narrative.

David Eaton employs a vast array of keyboards which include the mellotron and synthesizers adding atmosphere and ambience throughout.

The opening epic segues into *Archway of Tears* which in turn segues into *The Final Resting Place* and so on, drawing the listener into the story with the music superbly enhancing the overall experience.

The *Final Resting Place* is full of choral moments as the harmonies and guest backing singers deliver the ghostly feeling to great effect.

Next up is the title track which is more plaintive with piano prominent and lives up to the 'cinematic' nature for which *Anubis* are renowned. The basslines are glorious without being intruding and soaring guitar enriches the melancholic feel.

Weeping Willow, And I wait for my world to end, and *The Holy Innocent* follow beautifully with the latter track worthy to be included with the other epics on this album and again segues expertly into the final track.

All that is presents that epic in three parts; *Light of Change/The Limbo Infants/Endless Opportunity.*

For my own part, the keyboards are the real highlight from this epic with the grandeur of the mellotron pervading certain passages and synthesizer adding spooky moments.

The album was to receive a second release a few years later on the album *Lights of Change Live in Europe 2018.* Performed in the Netherlands in its entirety it presents a performance to rival the studio version. *Anthony Stewart* replaced *Nicholas Antoinette* on bass and is the only line-up change from the studio version.

Anubis is still active and have added immeasurably to their catalogue, but this album remains a personal favourite.

Arena – Contagion (2003)

John Mitchell is prolific and has appeared with such bands as; *It Bites, Frost, Kino, A, The Urbane* and of course *Arena*. *Lonely Robot* is the name adapted to release his solo material. *Mitchell* is also a producer and although vocal and guitar are his main instruments, he is also a multi-instrumentalist.

Arena released several albums, but this 2003 album is, in my opinion, the best in their catalogue.

The band at this stage were: *John Mitchell, Mick Pointer* (drums), *Clive Nolan* (keyboards), *Ian Salmon* (bass) and *Rob Sowden (vocals)* and individually had been members of; *Marillion, Pendragon, Shadowland* and *Mick Pointer Band. Rob Sowden* subsequently went on to play with *Solar* after quitting *Arena.* One could stretch a point and call *Arena* a 'neo-prog super-group'.

Contagion is of course a concept album from a story by *Clive Nolan,* with a title which is self-explanatory and a trifle un-nerving at the time (2021) of writing.

An album full of superb atmospheres and musicianship which flows through separate but inter-connected tracks with recurring themes and begs to be listened to as one complete piece. It does contain some very memorable and 'catchy' moments such as *Salamander* with the repeated chorus line *"burn like a moth to the flame"*. Add to this the overtly *Tony Banks* styled keyboards and you have one superb track which stands up to repeated listens. It segues into the instrumental *On the Box* brilliantly and without noticeably doing so.

Riding the Tide is the last of three instrumentals on the album and oozes prog at its very best with the dominant keyboards very much directing things.

Whether the band or individuals were unhappy with the finished product I cannot say but shortly after its release two eps were released. *Contagious* and *Contagium* (2003) added to the overall concept with additional tracks plus a remixed track on each ep; *Witch Hunt* and *Salamander* respectively.

Obviously fans went out a bought these eps but the 10th Anniversary edition of the album saw all three recordings amalgamated into one double cd incorporating some 90 minutes and fleshing out the concept over and above the original release. In my opinion, should one not have initially added this to their collection then this release is most definitely the one to get.

Contagion Max (2014) is both expansive and, if it's possible, a superior listening experience. The double disc was thoughtfully assembled inserting the ep tracks in just the right places while the booklet contains some extra bits and pieces.

In 2004 the album *The Cry* (1997) was released with bonus tracks. Those tracks are the seven new tracks from the complimentary eps for *Contagion*. Thoughtful of *Arena* as *Max* is difficult to source these days.

Arena remains one of the so-called 'neo-prog' giants alongside; *Marillion, IQ* and *Pallas* while not forgetting the other bands associated with the members of this release.

Argent – Nexus (1974)

Argent may not be among the leading contenders when one considers progressive rock but arguably *Nexus* was their pinnacle and an album considered worthy of inclusion in the genre.

Rod Argent had already established himself with the *Zombies* before teaming up with *Russ Ballard* (vocals and guitar), with *Jim Rodford* (bass) and *Robert Henrit* (drums) rounding out the line-up on for this release.

Best known for the hugely successful single *Hold your head up* (1972) *Argent* captivated the record buying public for a few years in the early 1970's.

The opening three tracks follow one another like one continuous piece and form a mini-epic. *The coming of Kohoutek/Once around the sun/Infinite Wanderer* are all showcases for *Rod Argent's* keyboards and represent his playing at its very best.

The album does have some 'cringe worthy' moments such as the slightly cheesy *Love* written by *Russ Ballard*.

Music from the Spheres a track written by *Argent/White* is a welcome return to the more prog styling. *Chris White* was a member of the *Zombies* and co-wrote five songs with *Argent* for the *Nexus* album but does not appear on it. At just over seven minutes it vies with the opening track for best on album and has some superb guitar with more than solid drumming. Vocals from *Ballard* are superb and keyboards are prominent.

Russ Ballard composed three other songs for the album with *Thunder and Lightning* considered the best of his contributions and vocally his best performance by far. His other two songs close the album. *A man for all Seasons* mirrors *Black Sabbath's* 'War Pigs' in sentiment if not style. Whereas *Sabbath* likens Generals to Witches *Ballard* suggests the 'man of war' is living Satan's law. *Gonna meet my Maker,* as the title suggests, is quasi-religious in nature but not a bad track with a strong vocal and driving rock motif.

Keeper of the Flame is another *Argent/White* song and is in keeping with their other songs on the album representing, as it does, the progressive element. Probably the most band-oriented track with no particular instrument or individual taking centre stage.

By the end of 1975 *Argent* had all but imploded but individual members would go on to other ventures however, not with the profile of the band and certainly not to the quality of *Nexus.*

Of all the songs in their canon one was to garner interest by the band *Kiss* when they covered *'God gave rock and roll to you'* and scored a huge hit. Many still associate the song with *Kiss* without releasing this *Russ Ballard* penned track appeared on the album *In the Deep* (1973) and the live recording *Encore* (1974).

Such is life.

Barclay James Harvest – Everyone is everybody else (1974)

Following their departure from EMI prog label Harvest *Barclay James Harvest* signed to Polydor with '*Everyone is everybody else*' proving their first album for the new label.

This is considered by many long-time fans and some critics as the absolute highlight in their catalogue. With a career spanning more than fifty years that is high praise indeed.

The line-up remained unchanged for the first ten years of their career and was: *John Lees* (guitar and vocals), *Les Holroyd* (bass and vocals), *Stuart 'Woolly' Wolstenholme* (keyboards and vocals) and *Mel Pritchard* (drums and percussion)

The album proved a gargantuan leap in many respects, not least of which was lyrically and most of these songs crossed over exceedingly well into their live set.

Child of the Universe had already been recorded for a projected solo album by *John Lees* – it was eventually be released – which was previously rejected by the band. The song is a lament to the children of our world and the dire situation many (unwittingly) had to endure daily. Beautiful guitar work from *Lees* accompanied by poignant lyrics concerning the children of; South Africa, Vietnam and Northern Ireland, but applicable universally, make this track a glorious opening to the album.

Negative Earth was a comment on the disastrous Apollo 13 space mission to the moon – the moon landing was aborted as technical problems ensued and returning the crew to earth became the priority. Famously *Holroyd* was at a loss to complete the lyrics and *Pritchard* lent a hand suggesting the line "here in syncopated time".

Paper Wings was another *Holroyd/Pritchard* song with some superb guitar from *Lees*. It could be seen as a precursor to a later song, *Suicide* from *Octoberon* (1976), in that both appear to be dealing with the same topic.

The Great 1974 Mining Disaster is a pastiche of the *Bee Gees* hit single *New York mining disaster 1941* (1967). Deconstructed by *Lees* it concerns itself with the miner's strike in the UK, it was not the first or last time such 'deconstructing' was employed.

Crazy City is a straight from the hip hard-edged song by *Holroyd* and remains one his very best.

See Me See You contains a quote from the *Beatles Hey Jude* but is a personal relationship song.

The piece de resistance comes with the culmination of the final three tracks which segue together beautifully. *Poor Boy Blues/Mill Boys/For No One* superbly end a superb album. The first two sounding like *Crosby, Stills, Nash and Young* with the harmonies before *For No One* concludes with an anti-war song highlighting sympathetic lyrics by *Lees* and his trade-mark guitar.

One song missing from the sessions was *Wolstenholme's Maestoso (A hymn in the roof of the World)* as the producer deemed it 'out of step' with the rest of the album.

It saw release some years later when *Woolly* issued his solo work but has been restored to its rightful place with the release of the excellent 2016 boxset of the album. Remixed, and also in 5.1 surround sound this is the definitive issue of their defining album '*Everyone is Everybody Else*'.

Barclay James Harvest may have come close over the years, but this remains (for many) their very best.

Kate Bush – Hounds of Love (1985)

The instantly recognizable voice of *Kate Bush* with the emotive high register captivated many with the impact of her first single success *Wuthering Heights* from the album *The Kick Inside* (1977).

Hounds of Love personally presents the epitome of her earliest work with a maturing artist who also gained a degree of mastery in the studio.

Bush was no stranger to the singles charts and two songs from side one on the original vinyl achieved success.

Running up that hill (A deal with God) has a pulsating drum beat and is possibly a 'drum machine' for which she gained a fondness – although *Stuart Elliot* is credited with drums. The title in brackets was to be the original title but EMI thought it might offend some listeners and suggested part of the lyric as an alternative. *Kate Bush* apparently insisted the original title be added in brackets.

Cloudbusting was the other single and has a similar feel to *Running up that hill* but with contributions from a string sextet plus various backing vocalist it has a lushness and ambience which make it a superior song.

Three other songs 'flesh out' side one (*Hounds of Love – The Big Sky – Mother stands for Comfort*) are all delivered in the inimitable style of *Kate Bush*. Vocally this album is a slight departure as there is less evidence of the high register with a richer timbre displayed.

Hounds of Love was also released as a single but did not attain the high chart position of the other two.

Side two of the original vinyl is a full-side suite broken into seven parts and is truly her prog-epic.

The Ninth Wave (And dream of sheep – Under ice – Waking the Witch – Watching you without me – Jig of Life – Hello Earth – The morning fog) is conceptual in nature and deals with one adrift and suffering dreams or hallucinations. As with most concepts it lacks total cohesion but it's the music and arrangements which make this epic so glorious.

Interestingly, there are various sound effects utilized and the helicopter on *Waking the Witch* is the same effect employed by *Pink Floyd* on *The Wall*. *Bush* did have a close professional relationship with *David Gilmour* so a little 'mate-ship' should come as no surprise.

Watching you without me is fantastic with a hypnotic theme running through and lyrically poignant in the style of *Wuthering Heights* and *the man with the child in his eyes.*

Jig of Life sees brother *Paddy* contributing not with an Irish instrument but the didgeridoo! As the title suggests it has an Irish feel with fiddles, whistles, bodhran and uillean pipes – an avenue *Bush* explored more than once.

Hello Earth includes a choir – *The Richard Hickox Singers* – which adds an almost operatic feel to the proceedings.

The Morning Fog is a little ambiguous regarding the fate of our antagonist. Did she survive or die and gain a spiritual release to rejoin the man in question? Listeners will draw their own conclusion.

The Ninth Wave enjoyed a second life when performed live complete with typical theatrics, lighting and projections and receiving release on *Before the Dawn* (2016). To sum up that performance in '*Bush*' parlance – Amazing!

Caligula's Horse – Rise Radiant (2020)

Arriving in the middle of a global pandemic *Rise Radiant* was a departure for *Caligula's Horse* inasmuch as the conceptual nature of their previous work had given way to 'stand-alone' songs.

The album art is glorious depicting a heavily antlered stag in a clearing and looking 'radiantly' toward a snow-capped mountain peak.

At this stage the band members were, *Jim Grey* (lead vocal), *Dale Prinsse* (bass), *Adrian Golbey* (guitar), *Josh Griffin* (drums) and *Sam Vallen* (lead guitar and everything else).

Equally majestic is the opening track *The Tempest* which gives the listener no time to sit down after pressing play before bursting through the speakers. Progressive metal at its best this is one of the standout tracks from an album I, personally, took a few listens to fully appreciate.

Slow Violence belies the title as it is anything but slow although the lyrics reveal some violence.

Salt sees *Jim Grey* singing 'achingly' before rising regally in the chorus. The band, in general are subdued after the first two tracks. *Sam Vallen* lays down some beautiful wistful and slightly bluesy guitar lines and the harmonies are top quality.

Resonate slows with an almost 'Beach Boys' vocal and relatively short – as is the respite.

Oceanrise picks up the tempo with excellent drumming and bass being under-pinned by a repetitive riff. As the album progresses appreciation grows for vocalist *Jim Grey.*

Valkyrie has a drum attack and with guitars 'ripping' in the metal-style prior the lead guitar taking centre stage. Lyrically it is probably the best track and again the vocals are superb.

Autumn is a wonderful track and one of the lengthiest. The guitars play in a subtle way offering a somewhat jazzy nuance in places clearly highlighting the virtuosity within *Caligula's Horse*. There is a feeling that you don't want this one to end. In a way it doesn't as it segues into the final track and takes on epic proportions.

The Ascent concludes the album, prior to two bonus (covers) tracks, in the same majestic way the album opened. Takes a few moments to get going but when it does it displays everything that is good in progressive metal. There are copious references to the album title in the lyrics, which are once again superb. *Vallen's* guitar cuts through again and makes the neck hair rise.

An album to blow away lockdown blues and one which gets better with the repeated plays it deserves.

Peter Gabriel's 'Don't give up' (1986) is the first of the bonus tracks and features *Lynsey Ward* as guest vocalist. They nail this track and do it more than justice.

The *Split Enz* song *Message to my Girl* (1984) receives great treatment from the band and varies just enough from the original to make it an interesting cover. I prefer *Jim Grey's* vocals to *Neil Finn's*.

Claypool Lennon Delirium – South of Reality (2019)

Les Claypool and *Sean Lennon* offer a surprising and brilliant album with the talent of *Lennon* surpassing expectations.

Little Fishes is lyrically obscure but on one level a comment regarding contamination of the earth and lamenting times passed when such issues weren't even considered. Musically it borders on progressive pop.

Blood and Rockets begins with an orchestral feel and this track is presented in two movements – *Jack Parsons* and *Too the Moon* (To is spelt too and not a typo).

Apparently about Jack experimenting as a young boy it follows him through to a debauched adulthood when he embraces the teachings of *Aleister Crowley.* Performed in a very upbeat style totally obscuring the message within. The song ends with the words "Do what thou wilt. Fly me to the moon"

South of Reality (Path of Totality) has some superb descending bass-lines alongside steady drumming. Vocals are good from both *Claypool* and *Lennon* but forget any comparisons to the latter's Father.

Boriska features heavy drums in a majestic song about a Russian boy *Boriska Kipriyanovich* who was born in 1996 and whose claim to fame came when he declared he was born on Mars in a previous existence.

Easily charmed by fools has a repetitive beat with chugging guitar and the song title repeated too often. It is a low point on the album but mercifully quite short.

Amethyst Realm offers the complete opposite and the most progressive sounding so far. Lyrically it feels almost like a lost *Edgar Allen Poe* story and bears some similarity to *The Raven.* Superb vocal and brilliant almost 'bluesy' guitar – difficult to know who is playing as both are credited with 'all instruments' – this is the best track on the album.

Toady Man's Hour reveals a man who obviously entered a life of crime only to be 'turned in' by either victims or accomplices. It is odd lyrically and musically while sung in a pseudo-rap style.

Cricket Chronicles Revisited is another two-part song (*Ask your Doctor* and *Psyde Effects*). There is an eastern feel to this song particularly with the percussion and use of the 'sitar'? Perhaps it is another *Edgar Allen Poe* moment.

Like Fleas would be almost humourous where the underlying lyrics not so serious. Delivered in an almost 'jocular' vaudeville style with a chorus concerning the dog shaking the fleas from its back but drawing comparisons to the parasitic nature of 'mankind' and 'Mother Earth's' eventual solution.

The biggest surprise of 2019 as, personally, I never considered listening to either *Les Claypool* or *Sean Lennon* previously.

Dead Letter Circus – The Endless Mile (2017)

Acoustically performed remixed and re-imagined songs from their catalogue this proved the second such release and is a pleasant and welcome diversion.

Containing the re-imaged 10th anniversary of their debut ep and five other tracks it represents a release which rates highly in their catalogue.

More renowned for a harder-edged progressive metal style this release met with some dissension from fans which is a little difficult to fathom as *Dead Letter Circus* are a very talented band and this is a clear indication of their virtuosity.

The Mile sets the scene for the entire album presenting an alternative version bordering on alternative pop/prog and is full of atmosphere.

Prior to the album's release an acoustic tour saw the band road testing and fine turning the eleven tracks with the added string section, keyboards and additional acoustic guitar.

It all makes for a lush rendering of well know songs but sounds like a totally new album and the departure from their usual style is starkly evident.

This is an avenue it is hoped they continue to explore with, perhaps, new material as opposed to back catalogue.

Dream Theater – Images and Words (1992)

Pull Me Under is not just the opening track but a pivotal moment in the history of *Dream Theater*. Released as a single, albeit edited from the original 8 minutes to placate FM radio, it catapulted the band into the consciousness of the record buying public. Receiving a second life (remixed 2007 version) in the 'tongue-in-cheek' compilation release *Greatest Hit (….and 21 other pretty cool songs)* (2008) it remains to this day their only hit single.

The first album to feature long-time and current Canadian vocalist *James LaBrie* with album art depicting songs from the album (a la *Genesis – Foxtrot* (1972) it is still a fan favourite.

Another Day was also released as a single but failed to emulate the success enjoyed by *Pull Me Under*.

Pigeon-holed as 'progressive metal' the band pushed those boundaries to extremes with subsequent releases and displayed a melodic direction previously lacking in much of the metal genre together with a virtuosity which was breathtaking.

One track stood head and shoulders above the rest and saw fans demanding a follow-up.

Metropolis Part 1 "The Miracle and the Sleeper" was an epic song which cried out for expansion and although it was sometime coming the fans were to be rewarded for their patience when *Metropolis Part 2: Scenes from a Memory* (1999) delivered the full concept.

Never resting on their laurels drummer *Mike Portnoy* and guitarist *John Petrucci* proved instrumental in their development with the former described as a 'workaholic' and 'control freak'.

Surrounded exhibited the more melodic side of the band and borders on a metal ballad with vocals to match. In much the same vein *Wait for Sleep* also displays *LaBrie's* incredible vocal range and dexterity while *Kevin Moore* adds beautiful piano.

If those two tracks are dominated by the vocalist, then '*Under a glass Moon*' is most definitely *Petrucci* pulling out all the stops with his guitar performing musical gymnastics!

Learning to Live is the closing epic and runs the gauntlet between progressive metal and straight-ahead rock with bassist *John Myung* shining throughout. A bass player of exceptional quality *Myung* was renowned among bandmates as a quiet and dedicated musician and an obsessed perfectionist.

The album lifted their profile amazingly but rankled *Kevin Moore* in particular as he appeared to shun the limelight and adulation which came with success. A few years later he departed citing the cliché 'musical differences' but in hindsight that is exactly what it was.

Dream Theater went on to enjoy – with some ups and downs along the way – an incredible and on-going career and become one of progressive metal's leading exponents.

Few of their albums in an expansive and varied catalogue met with fan indifference with the emphasis clearly on not repeating a winning formula but striving to stretch themselves as far as possible.

That sets the scene for the second album under consideration from the band as it is clearly a different animal altogether.

Dream Theater – Train of thought (2003)

Befitting the adventurous nature of the band *Train of Thought* is dark, menacing and brooding in equal measure.

By this stage *Kevin Moore* had been replaced by *Derek Sherinian* who was subsequently replaced by current keyboardist *Jordan Rudess*

The first indication is the album art. Stark black and white shot looking down a tunnel into a forest with a large human eye in the middle ground. The back cover is even more unsettling with a whirlwind above the eye of the storm which has a ladder coming from within.

As I Am begins with a very *Black Sabbath* sound which sets the scene for the entire album.

This Dying Soul is wonderfully heavy with *Portnoy* giving his drum kit a fair workout while *Petrucci's* guitar wails in sheer delight. The bass is so busy it's difficult to comprehend the speed at which *Myung* plays. *Sherinian* adds some adventurous keyboards and *LaBrie's* vocals are magnificent.

Endless Sacrifice slows proceedings somewhat but it is only temporarily and when the pace picks up again it is magisterial. At the halfway point the various band members seem to be in combat with each other for supremacy. *Sherinian* is supremely good on this track.

Honor Thy Father continues in typical heavy fashion with heavy drum and chugging heavy guitar. It is fast and furious.

The title is ironic as it is *Mike Portnoy's* comment on his relationship – not always sweet – with his stepfather but might also be questions faced (without answers) in any familial situation were a certain role is expected by society but not always lived up to. The fractured relationship is captured in the final verse with amazing progressive metal at its very best.

Vacant is short and almost a ballad. Plaintive and sombre it offers a little respite from all the heaviness.

Stream of Consciousness is a lengthy instrumental which appears to follow on from *Vacant* but is heavier and displays virtuosic playing from each band member. This song was revisited from a previous album (*Lines in the sand – Falling into Infinity* (1997)).

In the name of God hits a poignant chord with me. Growing up in Belfast and reaching my teenage years in the late sixties I was to witness the so-called 'troubles' which continued indiscriminately for over 30 years. People killing 'In the name of God' and justifying their actions was commonplace. Whereas no conflict or country is mentioned (some inferences are alluded to) the underlying message is that religious beliefs have been a foremost reason for violent acts perpetrated 'In the name of God'. Sadly, little seems to have changed.

Quite rightly the music is brooding and dark and very edgy in places with each member of the band stretching in every possible direction.

A superb ending to a brilliant progressive metal album which would see a reprise (of sorts) a few years later on the self-titled album released in 2013.

Progressive metal is rarely presented the way *Dream Theater* presents even though many have tried.

Still active, still relevant and still listenable – enjoy *Dream Theater.*

Electric Light Orchestra – No Answer (1971)

Released in the UK in late 1971 eponymously it was given its title when an American record executive instructed his secretary to phone the UK and obtain the album's title. She duly phoned but received 'no answer' and left a note informing her boss! The UK and US album covers have since become collector's items.

Roy Wood, Jeff Lynne and *Bev Bevan* are the core musicians (indeed their images are the only ones displayed) playing almost all the instruments and performing vocals. *Bill Hunt* (French horn and hunting horn) and *Steve Woolam* (violin) complete the line-up on their debut 'self-titled' album.

10538 Overture received release as a single which catapulted the album to chart success. Its impact was immediate and a far cry from the pop of their previous band *'The Move'* who had by all accounts earmarked the single as a 'b' side for *'The Move'*.

The overtly classical pretentions are carried through the entire album with *Wood* proving himself a multi-instrumentalist.

Look at me now has a sound more in keeping with later versions of the band and certainly more commercial than the single which was released.

Nellie takes her bow is similar but less commercial than 'Look at me now'.

Battle of Marston Moor (July 2ⁿᵈ, 1644) was a real historical event marking the first defeat by King Charles I and his Royalist forces against the Parliamentary army supported by Scottish allies and occurred in York. The music is 'war' like and backed by narration from *Roy Wood*.

Rumour has it that *Bev Bevan* thought so little of the track that he refused to play percussion – those duties were carried out by *Roy Wood.*

1ˢᵗ Movement with *Jeff Lynne* taking centre stage on acoustic guitar builds on the already classical feel to the album. It is the first of two instrumental tracks.

Mr. Radio again shows glimpses of the future direction the band would soon take and was also considered for single release.

Manhattan Rumble (49ᵗʰ St. Massacre) was not a historical event but ironically proved prophetic in that a massacre (49ᵗʰ Street Massacre) took place some years later in Los Angeles.

This instrumental is menacing and a little disjointed but remains the highlight for many, myself included.

Queen of the hours had the 'honour' of being released as the 'b' side to a later single '*Roll over Beethoven*' from their second album *ELO 2* (1973). What is obvious is the change of direction (which *Jeff Lynne* was 'orchestrating') between this track and those appearing on their second album.

Whisper in the night features *Roy Wood* on lead vocal and superbly ends this adventurous album with strings to the fore.

Wood soon departed and formed *Wizzard* while *Lynne* and *Bevan* carried the band forward.

The album '*On the third day*' (1973) saw a seven piece band offering the final installment of the overtly orchestral sound before scoring incredible international success with a more commercially and overtly pop sound.

Jeff Lynne later became a hugely successful producer.

Emerson Lake and Palmer – Trilogy (1972)

The third studio album but fourth overall from one progressive rock's most bombastic bands saw them take a well-deserved break from touring in late 1971 to work on *Trilogy*.

The front cover says it all. Their profile was high and the 'enhanced' picture of the three men appears as though they are joined together but looks can be deceiving as history was to prove things were far from 'united'.

Musically, though, the members of *ELP* were firing on all cylinders and this album continues were *Tarkus* (1971) left off.

The first three tracks flow as one. *The Endless Enigma (Part One) – Fugue – The Endless Enigma (Part Two)* commence with the sound of a heartbeat (later identified by engineers in a 2015 remixing as a bass guitar) and give way to piano and percussion. *Fugue* was *Emerson's* piano bridge between the two *Enigma* parts and relatively short. *Part Two* has some understated bass and guitar in an almost bluesy fashion. As usual *Lake's* voice is rich and unmistakably delivered as only he could. The newly acquired synthesizers add a different dimension and *Emerson* employs them to the full.

From the beginning features piano and acoustic guitar with some haunting lyrics thrown in for good measure and is again of fairly short duration.

The Sheriff is one of those amusing little songs which *ELP* had a habit of adding to almost every album (a la 'the Ringo song').

Hoedown sees *Emerson* doing what he did so well when interpreting others music. *Aaron Copland* was the original composer and its set to an arrangement credited to the entire band. Mainly a showpiece for keyboards it features some odd time signature drumming and pulsing bass.

Trilogy begins with tame piano and plaintive vocals but builds quite slowly until *Emerson* appears unable to rein in his natural exuberance and is joined by *Palmer's* superb drumming. Various keyboards are added as the song builds to a crescendo. *Lake's* vocals come across as somewhat detached as though he were standing well back from the microphone.

Living Sin remains one of the lesser-known pieces ever committed to vinyl by *ELP.* It is a straight-ahead piece of rock with vocals alternating between gruffness and finesse. Organ is prominent.

Abaddon's Bolero proved another slow building piece for which the drumming is very subdued – just keeping a steady beat. When *Emerson* finally fires up he throws everything at it including the proverbial 'kitchen sink'. It is a suitable ending to a more than suitable release, one which is revisited often.

Sadly 2016 saw the death of both *Keith Emerson* and *Greg Lake* but together with *Carl Palmer* they left an amazing legacy and one which is cared for with great affection by *Palmer's* tribute band.

Worth seeking out the 2015 re-release with the second disc offering an alternate stereo re-mix by *Jakko M Jakszyk.*

Enya – Watermark (1988)

The second album by *Enya* after her departure from *Clannad* proved immensely popular to a wide listening audience and bringing her international success as the single *Orinoco Flow* hit high in charts all around the world.

At a loss to pigeon-hole into one genre it would often be found in the 'new age' section at record stores. It is ambient with a Celtic feel (particularly vocally) but I shudder when I see it listed as 'new age'.

Enya was singer, songwriter and musician playing a wide variety of keyboards and synthesizers. *Watermark* was multi-layered with keyboard-oriented songs which established the sound for subsequent albums.

Cursum Perficio was apparently written on the tiles on *Marilyn Monroe's* front doorstep. The best translation from the Latin is "Your journey ends here".

On your shore references her hometown of Gweedore, County Donegal and in particular the beach of Magheragallon. Her grandparents are also buried here so the connection was quite emotional as is borne out in the song.

Storms in Africa is an absolute highlight from this delightful album along with *Storms in Africa (Part II)* the latter offered as a bonus track for the CD.

Miss Clare remembers is a title of a book by English novelist Miss Read, a book which *Enya* found appealing with its reference to English village life from a by-gone age.

Orinoco Flow opened side two on the original vinyl and proved pivotal on album sales – now estimated to be in excess of 8 million – and her popularity.

Evening Falls is a ghost story based on reality. The music is befitting the subject matter with that clear and evocative 'haunting' vocal.

River was a title suggested to *Enya* which she liked as the song has a gentle rolling ambience and apparently finished quite quickly in one take.

Longships may have been left over from her first album which was composed for the BBC TV series *The Celts*. Although the album is listed as self-titled (1987) it has become known as *The Celts*. Certainly, the Viking longships would have fitted in well with the overall theme.

Na Laetha Geal M'oige or to give it the English title "The brighter days of my youth", was a dedication to her grandparents to whom she was very close during her childhood. Extremely Celtic sounding with Uilleann pipes in evidence it is a beautiful ending to a wonderful album.

The CD version ends with the previously mentioned bonus track and subsequent pressing have expanded the original album. Whatever version you choose you will not be disappointed.

Eyefear – The Inception of Darkness (2012)

Eyefear presented a power metal style prior to *The Inception of Darkness* with a hard-edged sound typical of the genre but incorporating a melodic element with high octave vocals.

Their fifth and final studio album to date took everything to another level with progressive elements more to the fore and sits alongside work from the likes of *Dream Theater* or *Fates Warning* with complete ease.

The heaviness seldom eases up but is interspersed with some deft keyboards (piano in particular) and added atmosphere for good measure. It is, however, the vocals of *Danny Cecati* that are featured most prominently. Two guest vocalist mix things up a little. *George Kosmas* does his best metal growls here and there throughout the album while *Sarah Parker* delivers a more straight-forward vocal as counterpoint which steals the show on *The Inception of Darkness Part Two*.

The recurring piano motif lends to the feeling of a concept album of melodrama personified while virtuosic soloing takes a back seat most of the time apart from *Immortals* when we are treated to some high-powered guitar work from *Kosta*.

Evan Harris is a bass player who seldom gets the credit he deserves and his playing on some tracks is mind-blowing. Drummer *Zain Kimmie* does what he does best and his kit would require some 'TLC' after the sessions.

Rounding out the sound on keyboards is *Seb Schneider* and his touches just add flavour when required and some majestic moments.

Fates Warning – Disconnected (2000)

Fates Warning is a band of almost two distinct eras with their early material delivering power which allowed for little subtlety and was often one dimensional. Hard to pinpoint exactly when the more pleasing progressive element crept in – likely *A Pleasant Shade of Gray* (1997) – but with *Disconnected* it is more than apparent, perhaps maturity was a factor.

The core band currently was: *Ray Alder* (vocals), *Jim Matheos* (guitar) and *Mark Zonder* (drums) with *Joey Vera* (bass) and *Kevin Moore* (keyboards) rounding out the line-up.

Beginning with slightly distorted and sustained guitar blasts and ambient keyboards *Disconnected Part 1* immediately draws one in before segueing into *One*. *Ray Alder's* vocals are a perfect fit for music and *Zonder's* drumming is powerful and acrobatic.

So, drifts in on the back of understated keyboards but it is the superb bass work part way through that stands out with *Vera* and *Zonder* combing in gloriously rhythmic harmony.

Pieces of me lyrically the most memorable moment and the high register (which can be irritating with some vocalists) accentuates immensely to keyboards nuances.

Something from nothing is the first of two epic tracks and individual virtuosity is sacrificed with each band member contributing what was needed on this powerfully amazing track.

Still remains, another epic and represents the epitome of *Fates Warning's* transition from power metal to progressive metal. There are moments of sheer guitar mastery, some brilliant keyboards, superb drumming, bass playing at its best all topped by excellent vocals – may sound too effusive but this is a track which encapsulates the entire album.

Disconnected Part 2 begins and ends with the same howling guitar which opened the album. Between those are some atmospheric keyboards and sound effects. Not a vocal track but some human voices can be heard although it is difficult to follow exactly what is being said. When the guitar howling ends the album it has gone full circle and begs to be listened to again.

This album sits well alongside *FWX* (2004) with both being firm favourites from their catalogue. They are both well-structured albums with just the right mix of metal and progressive elements but 'Disconnected' will always be the first pulled off the shelf when a *Fates Warning* moment arrives.

Fish – Raingods with Zippos (1999)

A veritable 'who's-who' joined *Fish* on this album with *Steven Wilson* adding guitar to eight tracks among the most notable. *Steve Vantsis* (bass), *Tony Turrell* (keyboards), *Dave Haswell* (percussion) and *Dave Stewart* (drums) along with backing vocalists *Nicole King* and *Tony King* all contribute heavily too.

Tumbledown is a very upbeat and catchy pop/prog song and (lyrically) where the album title is taken from.

Mission Statement follows in similar fashion but lyrically *Fish* is in great form drawing parallels between the 'haves' of the world and the 'have-nots'. Lines such as "All it takes is kindness and a little love and care. And this planet that we live on can be a heaven we can share" are typical. He does not shy away from the need to delve inward and do some changing ourselves.

Incomplete is a beautiful ballad with counter-point lead vocal shared with *Elisabeth Antwi*. It explores relationships and the expectations when one embarks on a relationship against the reality of living it.

Titled Cross and *Faith Healer* are both solid with the latter being a cover of the 1973 *Sensational Alex Harvey Band* song.

Rites of passage, is a progressive mini-epic with superb atmospheres and strings by *Mickey Simmonds* and *Davey Crichton* respectively.

The final track is the crowning glory and a six-part epic which highlights *Fish* in full progressive rock mode.

Plague of ghosts has all the elements of earlier songs with spoken parts in that unmistakable Scottish brogue.

Beginning with plaintive vocal and sound effects it conjures up images of vacant rustic spaces and becomes more obvious in the lyrics. Indeed darkness is elaborated on in the section '*Digging Deep*'.

Chocolate Frogs is spoken word (mostly) and one can't help but think back to early *Marillion* and *Misplaced Childhood* (1985) in particular. Naturally a few Scottish terms are thrown in such as 'voddie' (vodka).

Waving at stars has a lyrical feel like the come-down aftermath of a live concert and the emptiness one would feel after all the adulation.

The penultimate section *Raingod's Dancing* appears a flow-on with the feeling of emptiness explored again.

The wake-up call (make it happen) and just about everyone who appears on the album seems to contribute to this final section. It again appears almost autobiograph-ical with some redemption but still lingering doubts exist. It would not be *Fish* if the lyrics were transparent!

Fast forward twenty years with *Fish* contemplating musical retirement after a few years of personal trauma. He has also delivered on his final album *Weltschmerz* (2020) which given the trauma is well titled.

His catalogue is awash with great music and he has given of himself so much over the years that it seems right to wish the man well in his future endeavours and thank him for some amazing memories.

Genesis – Foxtrot (1972)

This was the moment when *Genesis* started to see 'some' reward for the years of hard toll and daydreams, a turning point in their fortunes – although financial stability was still a few years away.

Foxtrot had everything and more including an epic which is still considered by many as the best of its kind.

Watcher of the skies is a cautionary tale but in time honoured fashion the lyrics can be interpreted several ways. Is this God rejection or acceptance? Is it visitors from another planet delivering a warning concerning our abuse of the earth? Indeed, interpreting lyrics was a favourite past-time among listeners during the early days of progressive music. Musically this was a song which transferred to the live setting with (or so it seemed) comparative ease.

Time Table is totally unambiguous and is a piano-led tale from a bygone age when things seemed so much simpler. Equally it lays down humankinds need to triumph over another race or religion in order to feel superior.

Get 'em out by Friday is gloriously amusing with *Peter Gabriel* voicing several characters in a tale of greed and the need to utilize every available space to squeeze in tenants. The song goes through several time changes and melodies before declaring our greed for material gain cannot be measured alongside spiritual contentment – a theme returned to more than once by *Gabriel*.

Can-Utility and the Coastliners, probably the weakest song on a good album, does have its moments. The referencing of King Canute displaying his fallibility in reaction to undeserved praise is priceless.

Side two on the original vinyl saw the greatest prog epic ever committed to record and one which still makes appearances on a regular basis when prog's greatest songs are considered.

Horizons, a short acoustic guitar piece by *Steve Hackett* highlighted what a brilliant musician he was/still is.

Supper's Ready has been performed live several times and still receives an amazing audience response. With references to; *The Musical Box*, Narcissus, Winston Churchill and the Christian bible book of Revelation (or Apocalypse) it had many scratching their heads. In reality it should not have worked but it did so wonderfully.

It begins with a sequence of events based on 'reality' and depicted in the cover art with "six saintly shrouded men". It has been revealed that it was a drug experience which drove the lyric.

The album art also depicted a female figure with a fox head and long red dress taking refugee from a hunting party. Famously *Gabriel* appeared on stage dressed in similar fashion wearing one of his wife's dresses. It was unveiled in Dublin to the surprise of the audience and, equally the band members.

The album is representative of *Gabriel-era Genesis* and the virtuosity of *Tony Banks, Mike Rutherford, Steve Hackett* and *Phil Collins* is evident throughout – not just this epic – the entire album.

A few years later and *Genesis* lost their theatrical front man and *Collins* would slowly introduce his stamp on the band. The arguments regarding which era truly represented the band continue unabated but financially the *Collins-led Genesis* flourished to become stadium fillers internationally.

Genesis – Wind & Wuthering (1976)

The second studio from the *Collins-led Genesis* after the departure of *Peter Gabriel* and the last to feature *Steve Hackett* was also the last to contain a full-on progressive feel. *Wind & Wuthering* is sadly neglected when considering their catalogue.

Eleventh Earl of Mar highlights the fact that *Collins* was yet to find his voice and certainly – as he later made quite clear – the lyrical content was not always to his liking. He did not feel he could offer a song the emotion it deserved when singing about 'mice' or fictitious 'Earls of Mar'. Nonetheless the song is a good opening and followed by the equally lengthy *One for the Vine* which is pure *Genesis* with *Collins* sounding uncannily like *Gabriel. Banks* shines of this track with his trademark keyboards evident.

Your own special way is a superior performance from the vocalist and given it is a precursor of the more commercially and romantically tinged ballads for which he was to become renowned, it is no surprise.

Wot Gorilla? The first of three instrumentals from the album is better than the name suggests. Drum and keyboard-led with deft touches on guitar from *Hackett* and *Rutherford* it was to find its way into their live set.

All in a mouse's night is the song which was to solicit the caustic remarks from the singer regarding lyrical content – on this song it's hard to disagree with him. *All in a mouse's night* may never make a top-fifty all time *Genesis* poll by fans but it really was not all that bad.

The last four songs on the album are superb and flow so well together bringing an end to *Hackett's Genesis* studio career with a flourish.

Blood on the rooftops opens with beautiful acoustic guitar and builds quite slowly with wordplay that their former singer would have embraced with relish.

The other two instrumentals follow, *Unquiet slumbers for the sleepers* and *In that quiet earth,* and segue seamlessly with the latter more driving and rockier. *Rutherford's* bass is particularly dominant in this song but he was never a showy player – perhaps too economical at times – and this outing does his playing style justice. *Banks* is also in fine form and again the live setting lifted these instrumentals over and above the studio versions.

Afterglow segues again making this a trilogy of exceptional quality with lyrics to match – reflected by the best vocal performance on the album.

As an album it is often over-looked and after this the commercial and more financially rewarding period of the bands career began, elevating *Genesis* to international stardom.

Prog was to raise its head from time to time on subsequent albums but not to the quality of *Wind & Wuthering.*

Gentle Giant – The Power and the Glory (1974)

Even in progressive rock circles *Gentle Giant* were an enigma. They sounded like no-one else with their intricate music and vocal harmonies (often 3 or 4 part) and lyrics to ponder over. They had an embarrassing and rich amount of talent with, arguably, three multi-instrumentalists in the line-up.

Derek Shulman, Ray Shulman, Kerry Minnear, Gary Green and *John Weathers* appear on the album and play all instruments with compositions by *Shulman/ Shulman/Minnear.*

The power and the glory is, for many, the crowning glory in a rich and varied catalogue and proved even more popular when re-issued in 2014 with mixes by *Steven Wilson* including a DVD 5.1 surround – this is the version to own.

Proclamation is one of those songs the untrained ear has difficulty spotting the time changes. It is gloriously quirky and one which the band would revisit more recently in a 'reunion' albeit on-line.

So Sincere probably represents *Gentle Giant* at their very best with the harmonies and musical starts and stops with lovely cello.

Aspirations, presents a jazz and blues influenced song with bass and organ dominating and laid-back vocals.

Playing the Game is as straightforward as *Gentle Giant* got on the album but even then, it's difficult to keep up with the myriad time signature changes – subtle though they are. Halfway through it becomes a whole other song entirely with a medieval feel before a heavier rock infused passage and bluesy organ combining with thumping bass prior to returning to the main theme.

Cogs in Cogs opens with keyboards and bass battling with each other as if racing to an imaginary finish line before the vocals kick in. Sung with a speed to match the music and with the bass playing the pivotal role it is a superb track.

No God's a Man highlights those wonderful harmonies but lyrically it is ambiguous given the title – at least to these ears.

Given the relatively short time taken (by today's standards) to complete the album it is totally mesmerizing and unfathomable. *Gentle Giant* did not indulge in long jam sessions and used studio time economically, but the results are incredible.

The Face is typical of the musical excursion they would sometimes undertake, and this achieves the quirkiness and musical virtuosity associated with the band.

Valedictory references *Proclamation* and ends the album with aplomb.

For whatever reason the original album did not include *The Power and the Glory*, but it is included in the aforementioned reissue as a bonus track.

Gentle Giant may not have achieved the success in commercial terms that they deserved but gathered a devoted fan base which is still actively supportive while drawing in a newer and younger group of followers. That is a validation of the complex and timeless music they performed and the fact it has taken some all this time to fully appreciate speaks volumes of their forward thinking and progressive mindset.

Haken – L-1ve (2018)

Superb live collection from a concert in Amsterdam spanning two CDs and two DVDs – the first being the full Amsterdam concert from 2017 while the second is *Live at the Prog Power USA 2016* – is exceptionally well presented in an mind-blowing box set.

It may have been easier to select one of *Haken's* studio albums and there is not one which would have been missed off, but this live set is just remarkable.

The progressive and melodic metal style of the band is one that offers a pleasurable departure from the likes of *Dream Theater, Fates Warning* or *Spock's Beard.*

The first cd skips around their catalogue opening with *Affinity* from the 2016 album of the same name but the ultimate performance is taken from *Aquarius* (2010) and presents a superb epic of 22 minutes plus wrapped-up as the *Aquamedley.* Naturally it will never be released as a studio version so this jump back in time to their first album does it more than justice.

Ross Jennings is an amazing vocalist with the band totally 'on fire' and not missing a single beat.

The second cd includes the incredible *Cockroach King* from *The Mountain* (2013), with those superb harmonies sounding even better live, as well as the epic 23+ minute *Visions* – the titular title from their 2017 release. The performance just gets better as it progresses, but the best is still to come.

The first DVD presents the *Full Amsterdam Show* and is an audiovisual experience worth savouring every minute of. The audience interaction is truly worth seeing as they show their appreciation throughout the entire performance but, naturally, save their greatest for the stupendous *Aquamedley.*

DVD 2 is a much shorter performance from *Prog Power USA 2016.* The tracks selected are a real bonus as none was performed during the Amsterdam concert making this a further treat.

The DVD also contains three music videos (*Initiate – Earthrise – Lapse*) and offer even more 'bang for your buck' as only *Earthrise* is performed live.

So hats off to *Ross Jennings* (vocals), *Charlie Griffiths* (guitar), *Conner Green* (bass) *Richard Henshall* (guitar and Keyboards) *Diego Tejeida* (keyboards) and *Raymond Hearne* (drums) not just for the exceptional performance but for assembling a box-set which is value for money and with the fans firmly in mind.

Following this beautiful set the band have issued a further two studio albums which are in keeping with their catalogue; *Vector* (2018) and the aptly named *Virus* (2020).

The latter has a five-part epic – *Messiah Complex* – which references *Cockroach King* and something many fans have looked forward to.

Horslips – The book of Invasions (1976)

The Irish progressive folk/rock band had a few years of high profile before selling their collective soul to a more commercial sound. This album is the absolute highlight in their canon.

The book of Invasions is also known as *A Celtic Symphony* with the music presented in the Celtic symphonic tradition of three principal categories of song (the joyous strain, the lamenting strain and the sleep strain) and delves into Irish folklore surrounding a story regarding a stolen instrument 'the Mighty One's harp'.

It does not matter whether one grasps the story or the musical tradition as the mix of rock, pop and folk tinged with progressive leanings is glorious and a forerunner of groups like *Clannad* with the Celtic feel.

Their contemporaries were, *Jethro Tull, Steeleye Span* et al but *Horslips* boasted a greater tradition to call upon.

The First Movement is in eight parts with *Trouble with a capital 'T'* and *Sword of Light* being the highlights. The former had a 'catchy' chorus but not 'catchy' enough to make headway as a single.

The Second Movement is less rocky and more in the traditional Celtic style with a ballad referencing *My Lagan Love*.

The Third Movement marks the final battle to retrieve the harp but ends in an abrupt and chilling *Ride to Hell*.

Progressive folk never enjoyed the success of 'rock' but in their time *Horslips* managed to release several wonderfully crafted albums and garner plaudits from critics and fans.

It Bites – Map of the Past (2012)

One of several projects/bands featuring the talents of *John Mitchell.*

A second look at *John Mitchell* with *It Bites* and this was my introduction to *Mitchell* and remains a firm favourite.

John Beck (keyboards), *Lee Pomeroy* (bass) and *Bob Dalton* (drums) complete the band for an impressive and (to date) last album from *It Bites* with *Mitchell* apparently concentrating on *Frost** at present.

A concept album which looks at the past through photographs it proved a departure for the band and met with some disapproval from fans – some seeing it as weaker and less accessible than previous albums.

The concept is completed by the booklet and disc design with the latter very retro in nature. Each song is accompanied by a photograph and offer sad poignant and sometimes blinkered views – befitting one leafing through old photographs.

Man in the Photograph is typical of what follows, and the spectre of war looms large in these songs.

Wallflower is melancholy and the picture of the beautiful young woman dates it to around early 1900's. She is of course a "wallflower" tending to her garden and shyly drawing away from others.

Map of the Past is depicted by a photograph of the band treated to look old. Musically, like the other songs, it is performed with aplomb and the harmonies outstanding. Some superb guitar breaks in halfway through and the overall feeling is upbeat.

Flag returns to the theme of war with the picture depicting a recruitment poster for WWI. The frenetic guitar introduction gives way to regular drum patterns and heavy bass with some retro sounding keyboards and is the rockiest track so far.

Cartoon Graveyard and once again the picture is the four band members this time as cartoon figures. Slightly humourous but the weakest moment – "don't want to end up a cartoon in a cartoon graveyard"!

Send no flowers along with *The last escape* offer the best two tracks on the album musically and lyrically.

Fittingly *Exit Song* is the final song with the picture again one of the band, or rather four separate pictures. *John Mitchell* looks every bit the WWII sergeant he portrays.

Patience is the order of the day with this album, it will yield a beautiful – and yes different – sound than previous albums but the time is well worth the effort.

IQ – The Road of Bones (2014)

It was a very difficult decision when choosing one album from *IQ*. After some pondering '*The Road of Bones*' is the album to introduce anyone to the delights of *IQ*.

Their early material bordered on pop/prog and was quite lightweight but as they matured and experimented more, so the standard rose and with '*The Road of Bones*' they hit an artistic high.

Peter Nicholls is 'the voice' of *IQ* and as history clearly shows he was hard to replace. On this album he and the band – *Michael Holmes* (guitar), *Tim Esau* (bass), *Neil Durant* (keyboards) and *Paul Cook* (drums and percussion) – are totally complimentary.

This is a two disc set with disc one the intended album and disc two a series of tracks considered demo's but are anything but. Essentially one receives two complete and different albums.

The five tracks on disc one are all lengthy and infused with *IQ's* trademark sound since the arrival of *Ever* (1993) which began an incredible run of albums expanded with experimentation and a more progressive sound.

Without Walls is the absolute epic from the album with all the prog accruements in place and with typical obscure *Nicholls* lyrics – he has become the modern equivalent of *Jon Anderson (Yes)*. The theme and tempo change several times and even resonates with some early '*Yes*' while exhibiting a modern feel.

I am reminded of *Harvest of Souls* from *Dark Matter* (2004) with the overall structure – plus the album covers have a similar feel.

Until the End rounds out the album with a mini epic to equal anything the band has recorded previously. It is atmospheric, experimental and heavier when required and fairly keyboard oriented.

Disc two contains six songs of stunning quality to rival the *'The Road of Bones'* and it's worth considering this purchase. There appears to be several versions with one offering live tracks but the studio tracks represented here really do feel like another album altogether and offer great value for money with a combined duration close to 50 minutes.

Knucklehead is a great opening track with understated acoustic guitar and *Paul Cook's* work some of his best. Atmospheric and lush with the right amount of rock infusion it is a brilliant track.

1312 Overture references the *1812 Overture* by *Tchaikovsky* and is the only instrumental over the two discs. Imagine *ELO* and *ELP* combining, and you may get some idea of the sound.

Constellations, is the stand-out from this set and the epic track. Descending drum patterns dominate and the bass playing by *Tim Esau* is mesmerizing.

Fall and Rise – Ten Million Demons – Hardcore round out the album while continuing the high quality and virtuosity evident on both discs.

Fall and Rise is the pick of the three with the bass again coming to the fore and keyboards and acoustic guitar adding beautiful nuances.

Ten Million Demons has a retro ambience and a little *Pink Floydish* while *Hardcore* (another mini-epic) is a close rival to *Constellations* and almost sounds like an out-take from *Dark Matter.*

IQ's best album by a long stretch and that's saying something!

Jethro Tull – Songs from the Wood (1977)

First of the so-called folk trilogy the album draws on English folklore with some tongue-in-cheek lyrics. Depicting a tree stump on the back cover complete with stylus the entire album resonates with *Ian Anderson's* famed humour – "A singer of these ageless times – with kitchen prose and gutter rhimes" (sic).

Tull will never be accused of being boring and repeating winning formulae as they genre hopped from blues to progressive rock and explored many byways in between.

The trilogy was inspired after *Anderson* had received a book on British folklore as a Christmas present and read it with relish.

Joining *Ian Anderson* are *Martin Barre* (guitar), *John Glascock* (bass), *John Evan* (keyboards), *Dee Palmer* (keyboards) and *Barriemore Barlow* (drums and percussion).

Songs from the wood appropriately opens proceedings with an invitation to let them bring us songs from the wood. It also plainly sets the intended folk style.

Jack-in-the-green was performed solely by *Anderson* and is medieval in feel. It could well be a reference to the folklore figure 'the green man' who is symbolic in pagan tradition as the harbinger of spring or cycle of life.

Cup of wonder refers to Beltane's flower and has association in mythology with the green man and synonymous with the Gaelic tradition of spring – celebrated on May 1st.

Hunting Girl or the 'Huntress' also has connection to the green man as this mythological figure was sometimes known as 'the green woman'. *Anderson* exhausted the theme with these three songs, so it is little wonder he moved from spring to summer or is it winter?

Ring out, Solstice Bells the solstice – a druid celebration – occurs in both summer and winter but this song also received an airing on *Tulls Christmas album* (2003). It is inter-changeable, and it seems in this instance to be summer as the next song *Velvet Green* is also about 'romping' in summer delights and full of sexual innuendo.

The next two songs are set as summer gives way to autumn and Scotland in particular. *The Whistler* and *Pibroch (cap in hand)* both suggest the roving minstrel and mention instruments of Scottish heritage – the fife and Pibroch or bagpipes.

Fire at midnight completes the seasons as winter is a time for building a fire to keep out the chill. It also references whisky (whiskey) with the "golden toddy on the mantle" and "silken mist outside the window".

As far as the folk trilogy goes this album encapsulates the genre to the full and *Anderson's* meticulous attention to detail is obvious.

As a celebration of British folklore, it is a treat and the only other band to go so deeply into the tradition that come to mind was Ireland's *Horslips*.

Jethro Tull – Crest of a Knave (1987)

Ten years on from the folk adventure *Tull* are exploring hard rock and metal music after a three-year break due to *Ian Anderson's* throat condition.

Officially the band was now a core of three – *Ian Anderson, Martin Barre* and *Dave Pegg* and this adventure into a heavier sound was met with mixed reactions and one enormous controversy.

Nominated for a Grammy Award in the hard rock/metal category the band did not even attend the ceremony as the expected winner was between *Metallica* – *...And Justice for all* (1988) and *Jane's Addiction* – *Nothing's Shocking* (1988). They took it out and that obviously did not sit too well with *Metallica* as in an acceptance speech a few years later *Jethro Tull* were thanked for not releasing an album during the previous year.

Released simultaneously on vinyl and compact disc the latter has two extra tracks, *Dogs in the Midwinter* and *The waking edge*. A re-mastered release in 2005 also contained a bonus track *Part of the Machine*.

Heavier than previous albums it was difficult to categorise the music as 'hard rock' let alone 'metal', in fact some saw it as drawing on a more *Dire Straits* styling.

Steel Monkey was released as a single and faired reasonably well reaching top spot on some charts.

Thematically it draws most heavily on war although *Anderson's* penchant for including sexual innuendo remained unabated.

The album received some unfair criticism and had a number of real highlights with the single being high on the list.

Budapest was to be incorporated in their live set and is the most *Dire Straits* like song with guitar and keyboards which could have been lifted from *Love Over Gold* (1982). That said it is an amazing track and quite lengthy at around ten minutes – probably best on album.

Dogs in the midwinter marks one of the tracks not appearing on the vinyl release and one wonders why as it is relatively short and would easily have fitted without any serious compression issues. It is also more in keeping to the tradition and style of *Tull*.

The Waking Edge is the other non-vinyl track and is experimental with the emphasis placed on the flute with a little plaintive piano and beautiful acoustic guitar it is a worthwhile addition to the overall feel and sound.

Part of the Machine is the bonus cut from the 2005 reissue and more than worthy of a mention. It feels a little like *Budapest* part two and even more so when playing the two tracks back-to-back.

Crest of a Knave ranks highly in their canon and it is somewhat perplexing that it received some of the negative reviews it did not to mention the bewildering categorisation.

Tull would go on to explore electronica and world music but at this stage of the game their music did exhibit a harder edge.

Kansas – Leftoverture (1976)

Kansas has enjoyed a long and successful career releasing albums on a regular basis – a few of questionable quality – which have (generally) stood the test of time.

Leftoverture marks a personal introduction with their fourth studio album and would lead to adding a substantial portion of their catalogue to my library.

The album art is striking with an ancient scribe composing with quill and scroll and a grand piano in the background. The title was a portmanteau of 'leftover' and 'overture'.

It is notable that *Steve Walsh* co-authored just three songs although one of those was the epic *Magnum Opus*. It appears he was suffering 'writer's block', regardless this release is superb.

Carry on Wayward Son was released as a single and enjoyed regular airplay and heavy rotation reaching the number one position in America and still receiving airplay on classic rock stations. There is some wonderful harmonisation and the signature *Kansas* sound.

Steve Walsh, Kenny Livgren, Robby Steinhardt, Richard Williams, Dave Hope and *Phil Ehart* need little introduction to progressive rock fans with *Ehart* still occupying the drum stool and a driving force behind the current line-up.

The Wall starts with stellar guitar work and typical lyrics delivered with aplomb. The bass is solid, melodic and (fairly) high in the mix.

What's on my mind the shortest and least memorable track but has gone on to become a staple in their live repertoire. Guitar has some rocky intervention and again the harmony singing is glorious.

Miracles out of Nowhere is a real highlight with acoustic guitar and keyboards dominating early. *Ehart's* drums sound excellent and the added touches on violin make this a stand out.

Opus Insert and *Questions of my Childhood* are both excellent with a swirling feel but it is final two tracks which truly mark this album out as special.

Cheyenne Anthem begins with keyboards and synthesizers which lend an old western sound. Lyrically it outlines the original inhabitants of America and how they once were "mighty on the earth". A combination of drumming gives the impression of horses riding the prairie prior to the angelic voices and crescendo.

Magnum Opus the six-part epic and final track is a masterwork and seldom over the years bettered by any line-up of the band.

It almost feels like a continuation of *Cheyenne Anthem* with some *Yes* style guitar sneaking in. Some of the titles employed are a little mysterious such as *Father Padilla meets the perfect gnat* and *Release the beavers.*

This represents the early *Kansas* at their 'pinnacle' and is a track which changes tempo and direction several times keeping one absorbed.

The album received a second life when an anniversary tour saw it played in its entirety, recorded and released as *Leftoverture Live and Beyond* (2017) – an amazing performance of an amazing album.

Karnivool – Sound Awake (2009)

The second full-length studio album from Australia's premier progressive/metal band *Karnivool* presents as best in their short catalogue.

Ian Kenny (vocals), *Drew Goddard* (guitar), *Mark Hosking* (guitar), *Jon Stockman* (bass) and *Steve Judd* (drums and percussion) are joined by a numbers of guest musicians mostly performing vocal arrangements on *Goliath* in particular.

It stands apart from either *Themata* (2005) or *Asymmetry* (2013) as the most progressive sounding and band oriented. It is well documented that *Goddard* had much of their debut written and performed before the band were assembled. In essence they were sidesmen and that is why *Sound Awake* is much more satisfying – as heretical as that may sound to some.

The album art is amazing too depicting an orb surrounded by an aural glow against a dark background and resembling a human eye – *Sound Awake* was an inspired choice for the title.

Fairly well received on its release the album charted well in Australia and around the world while being nominated as Australian album of year. *Set fire to the hive* was released prior to the album as a single and did very well promoting the upcoming album.

Progressive, atmospheric, melodic with superb and complex musicianship it is an album to savour time and again.

Goliath boasts five additional vocalists while *Change* includes additional percussion and didgeridoo from *Sam Tilot Kickett* and *Umbra* sees *Jason Bunn* play viola.

Umbra is one of the highlights from an album bubbling with great moments. Virtuosic performances especially on acoustic guitar, bass sounds fantastic and high in the mix, vocals outstanding and drumming of highest quality.

All I know presents a song of immense poignancy as the plaintive and emotive vocals from *Kenny* shine but is followed by the shortest track – *The medicine wears off.* Featuring acoustic guitars and vocal it suddenly gets a little heavier before segueing into *The Caudal lure* which has a jazzy groove.

The final two tracks are of epic proportions with a combined duration over 23 minutes. *Deadman* appears to end around the ten-minute mark but just a few seconds of silence is followed by a re-worked version of *Change (part 1)* from *Themata* before segueing into *Change (Part 2).*

These two songs – better considered as one epic song – were to draw comparisons to: *Tool, Porcupine Tree, Muse* and *The Mars Volta.* Whereas it would be simplistic to do so it must be emphasised that *Karnivool* are unique and present their own sound in these tracks.

Deadman has excellent performances with *Grant McCulloch* brought in as an extra vocalist. The bass is remarkable and good enough reason to seek out *Stockman's* work with other projects, such as *Floating Me* (stylised as *FloatingMe*) from their eponymous album released in 2011.

Change is quite an eerie ending to the album and cinematic in scope with lots of soundscapes and time signature changes particularly with the drums as they appear to jump from 4/4 to goodness knows where and back!

Some band members are busy with other projects with *Kenny* touring heavily with *Birds of Tokyo* but hopefully a new album is on the horizon and one reflecting the sheer quality of *Sound Awake* would be welcomed.

King Crimson – In the court of the Crimson King (1969)

One cannot underestimate the impact *King Crimson* made with '*Crimson King*'. *Robert Fripp* (guitar), *Ian McDonald* (woodwind and keyboards), *Greg Lake* (bass and lead vocals), *Michael Giles* (drums and percussion) and *Pete Sinfield* who was credited with 'words and illumination' and formed, at least initially, an integral part in the band, presented an album which to this day is considered the first 'real' progressive rock album.

They were to present the album live as support to the *Rolling Stones* during a free concert at Hyde Park in London which ended up being a tribute to the recently departed *Brian Jones*. The *Stones* for ever after would seriously check-out their support act as *King Crimson* superbly presented their complex music to an unsuspecting public.

The iconic cover with the menacingly grotesque face was quite frightening at the time and coupled with the all-out assault of the opening track *21*st *century schizoid man* did, from that moment on, change everyone's perspective about what could be achieved.

Debuting on the British charts at number five behind the *Stones, Johnny Cash, a Motown Compilation* and sitting atop the *Beatles Abbey Road* it is patently obvious that this was a whole new ball game.

I talk to the wind is in stark contrast to the opener. Pastoral with a balladry sound it was nonetheless lyrically brilliant exposing a world-weary view regarding the impositions made on one.

Epitaph is presented in three parts and a song incredibly structured also highlighting *Sinfield's* imagination to the full but it is *Greg Lake's* delivery of the lyrics which still has the ability to amaze.

Moonchild, also in three parts, was a song of epic proportions but due to an extended middle section which – on the equipment of the day – was almost inaudible many people skipped over it. The equipment of today irons out these problems and re-mastered versions clearly bring out all the nuances missed at the time.

The court of the Crimson King including The return of the Fire Witch and The dance of the Puppets is quite a mouthful but more importantly quite an epic on which to end.

"Court" was a game changer with changing moods and atmospheric keyboards together with the story of the *Crimson King* and his *Court* painting an image of a powerful and domineering character who presided over a fearful regime. As the song progresses the lyrics inculcate the characters of the *Fire Witch* and the *Puppets* who are manipulated by the court jester. It is a convoluted story of power, wealth and dominion.

King Crimson toured the album to critical and commercial acclaim but as the tour continued cracks in personal relationships began to appear and the band split before the next album appeared. This tortured existence dogged *Crimson* and *Fripp* (in particular) as the 'on again off again' history of the band would have ardent fans almost tearing their hair out.

Such is the 'cult' though that some incarnation was always available to tour and record (spasmodically) and as of 2021 they remain 'active'.

Some to their subsequent albums rate well while some are easily forgotten but *King Crimson* set the bar high with their debut and struggled to repeat the formulae.

Lonely Robot – The Big Dream (2017)

Another *John Mitchell* project but with a difference as *Lonely Robot* is a *John Mitchell* solo project in all but name. *Mitchell* plays all instruments (that includes cello, Irish whistle, Celtic harp and harmonium) except drums which are performed by one of progressive rock's top drummers *Craig Blundell*. *Bonita McKinney* (vocals) and *Lee Ingleby* (narration) are the only other persons appearing on this album.

Mitchell also composed, recorded, produced, mixed and re-mastered the album – clearly a man of many talents.

The Big Dream is the second installment of a trilogy entrenched in a sci-fi tale of a stranded astronaut. This episode is, arguably, the best of the three.

Opening with the *Prologue – Deep Sleep* our protagonists awakens in a forest surrounded by creatures resembling the cast of a Shakespearean play (think A Mid Summer's Night Dream). It begins with subtle piano before breaking loose with superb drumming from *Blundell*. The narrator poses some philosophical thoughts such as wondering "what it must be like to go to sleep and never wake up".

The voices of *Mitchell* and *McKinney* when they harmonise is magical and the guitar solos and general guitar work highlight a guitarist under-rated. He's no slouch with the bass either. His keyboard touches also lend cinematic moments of beauty.

False Lights contains some ascending guitar patterns, but it is the drumming which stands out on this track. *Blundell* seems happiest when not performing in 4/4, displaying his skill and driving this song in various time signatures but mainly either 6/4 or 5/4.

The Divine art of being is built around another drum pattern which is evidence of the working relationship the two musicians share. The vocals are plaintive with guitar matching the 'aching' feeling.

The Big Dream is the longest track and one in which the narrator is heavily involved. The idea of going to sleep and never waking up returns and in fact is omnipresent on the album. Our protagonist is yearning to return and some lyrics from the first of the trilogy *Please come home* (2015) are reprised. The song overflows with a sadness obviously felt by the astronaut.

Hello World, Goodbye finds our astronaut resigned to his (seeming) fate while adrift in space and longingly viewing the Earth. The guitar solo which begins this track is spectacular and again the drumming is incredible.

Epilogue – Sea Beams has a 'baroque' style piano and the track leaves the protagonists fate 'in the air' and to be revealed in the final episode.

Under Stars (2019) brings the concluding part to this saga. Naturally it is best enjoyed by listening to the three albums in sequence.

I could have chosen any of the three as all are amazing, but *The Big Dream* is crammed with ethereal and cinematic moments alongside stellar performance from *Mitchell* and *Blundell* and neatly enhanced by *McKinney* and *Ingleby.*

Mitchell has released one more *Lonely Robot* album with *Feelings are good* (2020) and treads a much more 'earthly' path.

Manfred Mann's Earth Band – Solar Fire (1973)

Is it conceptual? It would be easy to draw that conclusion as this work is loosely based on 'The Planets – Gustav Holst'.

The album art is glorious depicting the night sky complete with solar flare. Apparently, it was simply and cheaply achieved by painting the scene on a piece of cardboard then pin-pricking it. Holding it up to a light the result is stunning.

Father of Day, Father of Night opens the album with this *Bob Dylan* cover – the only cover on the album – and was typical of *Mann's* interpretation when covering songs. It sounds nothing like the original and has some fantastic guitar work from *Mick Rogers* who also performs vocals. *Mann* performs on just organ and synthesizer with *Colin Pattenden* (bass) and *Chris Slade* (drums) rounding out this line-up.

In the Beginning, Darkness relates to the formation of life 'as we know it' and contains the phrase *Solar Fire* even though the titular song appears later and does lend some credence to recurring themes for those who like to think of this as a concept album.

Pluto the Dog is an instrumental track barring the annoying barking dog – must have been listening to *Seamus* by *Pink Floyd* at the time. It is a repetitive melody and thankfully quite short.

Solar Fire is under-pinned by stellar bass from *Pattenden* and (so it seems) female backing vocal which is most likely *Mann* with *Rogers* taking the lead.

Saturn, Lord of the Ring. Mercury the Winged Messenger a track written purely by *Mann* and obviously filled with his keyboards, particularly synthesizer, is as progressive as the *Earth Band* ever achieved. The over-blown title is the result of three easily identifiable tunes melded into one and totally instrumental.

Earth, the Circle Part 2 is strangely followed by *Earth, the Circle Part 1*. Both *Mann* compositions with the organ prominently displaying a jazzy feel and showcase his talent to the full. The two parts do not segue or even sound similar with Part 1 offering more lyrics and greater use of the synthesizer.

Joybringer was released as a single and charted well giving *Mann* his first hit since 1969. It was not included on the original album but one would assume it was the intention – perhaps the vinyl limitation prevented it from doing so or a reluctance to release a single which appeared on the album – that was rectified when it was re-issued on disc in 1998.

This version of *Manfred Mann's Earth Band* soon changed with the band achieving greater commercial success however, for many *Solar Fire* marked the pinnacle of the early band line-up.

Marillion – Script for a Jester's Tear (1983)

Marillion were among the vanguard for the so-called neo-prog movement during the 1980's and the line-up for their debut album was, *Fish (Derek Dick)* (vocals), *Steve Rothery* (guitars), *Pete Trewavas* (bass), *Mark Kelly* (keyboards) and *Mick Pointer* (drums). *Pointer,* a founding member, was soon replaced but was to further his career elsewhere and with great success.

Mark Wilkinson created the album artwork which was to be the start of a long and fruitful association with the band and *Fish* in particular. The Jester became synonymous with the first era (or *Fish* era) and continued a tradition from the earliest days of progressive rock when fans were poring over the album art for hidden clues to the songs.

Prior to the issue of their debut album *Marillion* released a 12" single *Market Square Heroes* (1982) with the B-sides *Three boats down from the Candy* and the epic *Grendel*. None made it to 'Script' but with compact disc technology in its infancy and yet to gain world-wide acceptance one wonders if these tracks were considered. They did receive release on the excellent compilation *B-sides themselves* (1988).

The album was released to critical and commercial acclaim attaining the number seven position in the UK and spending over six months in the charts. It also achieved platinum certification selling in excess of 250,000 units.

In total six tracks adorn 'Script', and all were performed live with *He knows you know* released as a single making the top 40. A second single 'Garden Party' did even better and broke the band to American audiences.

Script for a Jester's tear rightly is the opening track and, as with all tracks, the lyrics were penned by *Fish* who became widely renowned for the quality and, at times, personal nature of his lyrics. Musically it displayed the virtuosity which was soon to become synonymous with *Marilliion*.

He knows you know, the aforementioned single is the shortest track at just over five minutes. Emotive in the vocal delivery it also contributed greatly to reinvigorating the progressive rock genre.

The Web has some superb drumming from *Pointer* and the title was later used for a fanzine. *Mark Kelly's* keyboards are excellent and in keeping with the oft made comparisons with *Genesis*.

Garden Party the second single and a concert favourite saw fans enthusiastically join the refrain *"I'm Fucking"* – tellingly the line did not appear in the printed lyrics. A song full of sarcastic references to, as *Fish* perceived them, the elite and entitled from public school backgrounds.

Chelsea Monday seems, on face-value, to be a song about a personal relationship and directed to a particular person. It contains some stellar and under-rated guitar work from *Steve Rothery* while *Pete Trewavas* on bass takes the limelight toward the conclusion.

Forgotten Sons references the 'troubles' in Northern Ireland as witnessed on nightly news reports and indeed has *Peter Cockburn* playing the part of the newscaster while a re-interpretation of the Lord's Prayer is wittingly sarcastic. The best track by far on this outstanding debut was bettered in live performance with *Fish* offering an emotional and heart-felt introduction.

Marking the first of an unlikely trilogy that propelled *Marillion* to incredible success before the first incarnation imploded this represents an album as relevant today as on release.

Marillion – Brave (1994)

Steve Hogarth composed a fictional narrative for this concept album surrounding a factual event. The River Severn Bridge which connects south-west England to south-west Wales is a mighty span and become infamous for the number of suicides taking place. *Hogarth's* concept is the imagined story of a young girl found by police when she was spotted wandering the bridge looking lost and refusing to divulge any information.

Brave was brave in that at the time concept albums were considered passé and their label EMI needed something more commercial. There was nothing remotely like a hit single on the album.

It was not well received, and many fans failed to grasp the grandeur of the project and sheer musicianship on display. Released as a double vinyl it did nonetheless, at least initially, chart well but proved a 'slow-burner' taking time to assimilate all the nuances. As time has passed it has gained more optimistic reviews and a better reception from new listeners. In fact, *Steven Wilson* completed a re-mastering of the album in 2018.

The vinyl also had a double-groove at the conclusion which, depending on where the stylus landed offered two possible endings. One is positive while the other indicates a 'drowning' with continuous water sound effects.

The only personnel change from their debut album was of course, *Steve Hogarth* and *Ian Mosley* on drums and percussion who had been with the band since the departure of *Mick Pointer*.

Highly atmospheric in nature the tracks blend into one another as the outcome of the young girl is explored. It becomes a pointless exercise to present a track-by-track analysis as these need, indeed beg, the listener to follow the narrative from beginning to end.

Guitar passages are, in general, subtle befitting the overall 'feel' of the concept. *Hogarth's* vocals are plaintive and emotive barely rising to a high register but complimentary to the album theme and music.

EMI soon dropped the band and they signed to Castle but become disillusioned with the lack of support and poor marketing.

The 'brave' decision to commence their own label and seek 'crowd-funding' through the internet site not only set a precedent others would follow but was evidence of the high esteem in which the band were held.

Anoraknophobia (2001) proved the resulting album which EMI agreed to distribute and market.

Since then they have released some remarkable albums; *Marbles* (2004), *Sounds that can't be made* (2012) and *F.E.A.R.* (2016) with latter seeing a welcomed return to the UK charts.

At the time of writing *Marillion* have launched a pre-order crowd-funding appeal for their 20th studio album '*An Hour before it's Dark*' which is due for release 2022.

Touring has also been planned but the pandemic has had a devastating effect on a band which relies on touring income and merchandise sales so once again they appeal for help to fund the tour.

Fans of the band come from a wide demographic and have supported the band in the past – I have little doubt that this will happen again and that the appreciation of *Marillion* will be shown to all – one way or another.

The Moody Blues – Days of future Passed (1967)

Is this the first fully-fledged progressive rock concept album? I would argue that it is a genuine contender but more importantly this album launched the band forward when their fortunes seemed to be waning.

The Moody Blues had been essentially an r 'n' b band and despite one hit single *Go Now* (1964) had prior to the release of the album been touring working men's clubs in the midlands and north of England and appeared to have 'run their race'.

Signed to Decca they were invited to work on a pop/ rock interpretation of *Antonin Dvorak's Symphony No.9 in E Minor* (popularly known as the *New World Symphony)* as a testing ground for the companies 'Deramic Sound System (DSS)' and to help pay off their huge debt to Decca.

Decca appointed *Tony Clarke* as producer and the *London Festival Orchestra* conducted by *Peter Knight* joined the band in the studio.

Justin Hayward (vocals), *John Lodge* (bass), *Mike Pender* (keyboards), *Ray Thomas* (flute and vocals) and *Graeme Edge* (drums) proved to be the 'revamped' version of the band by 1967.

The inclusion of the 'Mellotron' and a more psychedelic sound together with a philosophical and mystical approach to the lyrics saw the band turn the opportunity on its head to produce an album of their own material to work on the concept of 'a day from sunrise to sunset'.

The day begins and *Dawn: dawn is a feeling* saw the collaboration between group and orchestra working well under the auspices of *Tony Clarke* and the project was kept from record executives as they were left to work without undue interference.

The Morning: Another Morning and *Lunch Break: Peak Hour* continued with the idea of a passing day.

The Afternoon (Tuesday?) saw release as a single and became known as *Tuesday Afternoon*.

(Evening) Time to get away rounded out the middle part of the day as the 'concept' took on shape and purpose.

Evening a) The Sun Set b) Twilight Time both carried the overtly mellotron driven album toward a conclusion. *Hayward's* vocals proved a vast improvement from the previous singer *Denny Laine* – later to gain popularity as part of *Paul McCartney's Wings*.

It is without doubt that the final track on the album was a pivotal moment in the *Moody Blues* fortunes. A tune penned by the relatively young *Hayward* with insightful lyrics beyond his years, lush orchestration and spoken word it became a concert favourite and latter-day touring line-ups still perform it with aplomb.

It would be fair to say that some of the album sounds dated and some of the spoken word and lyrics twee, but it worked – much to the astonishment of Decca executives who reportedly sat wide-mouthed after hearing it for the first time. The now famous remark "you can't dance to it" was apparently uttered more than once.

The only problem facing all was that the *Beatles* issued *Sgt Pepper's Lonely Hearts Club Band* around the same time and *Jimi Hendrix* was riding a successful wave in re-interpreted blues/rock.

Still, it was a landmark which has grown in stature and importance rightly deserving a place in anyone's top albums of all time.

Opeth – Heritage (2011)

True to say this was not everyone's choice and as an album, it proved divisive with fans but, in hindsight, propelled the band forward to produce amazing work to wide acclaim since.

My initial introduction was *Blackwater Park (2003)* and proved pivotal to adding more *Opeth* to the collection but nothing was to prepare me for what lay in this album.

Mikael Åkerfeldt wrote all the songs as well as being the vocalist and producer alongside *Steven Wilson* – a collaboration which has yielded some stellar work.

The first thing that becomes obvious is the total absence of metal growl in favour of a more melodic and emotional delivery. Secondly the metal element gives way to passages of piano, acoustic arrangements and a heavy rock style.

The album opens with the title track and is purely grand piano performed by *Joakim Salvberg* with no other contribution on the entire album. It is in the classical style and leaves one wondering where they may have heard it previously. Nothing comes to mind.

The Devil's Orchard has some beautiful acoustic guitar but is a builder and grows heavier as it progresses.

I feel the dark and *Slither* is the first indication of the prog/metal styling. As the latter reaches a conclusion the mood changes totally and is played out on acoustic guitar in a quiet fashion.

Nepenthe is similar to the work of *Steven Wilson* and his influence is rarely so open but he doesn't actually play on the album at any stage.

Haxprocess begins with a jazzy fusion and subtle nuances before a very laid-back acoustic passage. *Martin Axenrot's* drumming is superb as he skips before and after the beat in jazz mode. Bass guitar is notably higher in the mix on this song with *Martin Mendez* performing brilliantly. It rounds out with *Gilmour-esque* electric guitar that drifts to the end of the track.

Famine starts with atmospherics and effects with the mellotron clearly discernable. Around the three-minute mark the pace picks up with the drumming roaring in and wonderful keyboard passages from *Per Wiberg*. Experimental in places heavy in others and subtle when required it is by far the best track on the album.

The lines in my hand and *Folklore* continue with an eclectic mix of rock/jazz/experimental elements with *Folklore* living up to its title and acoustic guitar being the prominent instrument. The bass has a deep rich sound and must be assumed to be upright bass. Some vocal treatment is also evident.

Marrow of the Earth concludes as the album opened – instrumentally. The acoustic guitar is the lead instrument, but keyboards slowly creep in with a little discernible 'humming vocal' before the end.

It doesn't stretch the imagination to understand why many older fans found this not to be to their liking however can an artist or band truly align themselves to the progressive genre and not progress?

Heritage stands alone in the catalogue of *Opeth* and marked them out as an adventurous and progressive band. It is a wonderful album that should be embraced by all professing to love progressive music.

Pendragon – Masquerade Overture (1996)

Pendragon are another leading light from the 'neo-prog' movement with longevity and willingness to progress beyond their early styling very evident.

Symphonically progressive in nature it captures the early prog style of *Genesis and Pink Floyd* (among others) and builds on it to offer a more updated approach to sublime effect.

Nick Barrett (vocals/guitar), *Clive Nolan* (keyboards), *Peter Gee* (bass) and *Fudge Smith* (drums) are joined by a cast of backing vocalist to create a pseudo-operatic feel to the album particularly in the opening and title track.

As good as gold follows and displays a very eighties neo-prog keyboard driven song complete with haunting guitar and more than competent drumming. *Nick Barrett's* lyrics are excellent with enough hooks to make them memorable.

Paintbox is a beautiful and plaintive song. One can visualise the isolation of the artist as they sketch out their vision. Guitar and keyboards dominate this song which became a fan favourite and received various re-imaginings. This song resonates as I personally have a few artistic people in my extended family and always think of them when I hear this song.

The pursuit of excellence has a 'Caledonian' element which permeates and nowhere more so than in the lyrical delivery. Short but superb track and wonderfully produced.

Guardian of my Soul is atmospheric with virtuosity extremely apparent especially from *Nolan's* array of keyboards. The backing vocalists are heard in their more natural styling to great effect.

The Shadow, a lengthy track which never loses its way begins with soft tinkling piano and sombre vocal before slowly building toward a guitar and bass section of sublime quality. *Peter Gee's* bass lines are melodic while the keyboards duel with lead guitar as the song picks up even more pace. *King of the Castle* makes an appearance here and was released as a separate track. *Nick Barrett's* Fender Stratocaster soars and weeps making a sound unique to the model.

Masters of Illusion saves the very best to last and this has everything the symphonic progressive rock fan would ever want to hear in a single song. Fantastic lyrics and vocals, bass, keyboards, guitars and drums all combining cohesively. Changes in mood and tempo hold the attention of another lengthy offering with, here and there, a sound similar to *Fish* era *Marillion* but only just discernible.

Pendragon went on to produce heavier and harder-edged albums, but this is a fine example of their symphonic and melodic style and direction, standing the test of time wonderfully.

Phideaux – Doomsday Afternoon (2007)

The second part of a trilogy which became known as the 'eco-terror' trilogy *Phideaux Xavier* (born Scott Riggs) is an American television director and composer.

The first part *the great leap* (2006) was issued the previous year, but it was to prove another infuriating eleven years before the concluding two disc release of the final part *Infernal* (2018).

Doomsday Afternoon has often been selected as the best of the three and with good reason.

Previously *Phideaux's* music is best described as accessible progressive pop and indeed was well received. It would also be true to say that *the great leap* fell into this category. *Doomsday Afternoon* proved to be 'a great leap' as it plays more like a concept album of epic progressive proportions with a duration of around 65 minutes.

Phideaux Xavier (vocals, piano, moog, 6 & 12 string guitar) is joined by an eight-piece band, small orchestral ensemble and several guest musicians which included *Martin Orford (IQ)* (synthesizer) on *Formaldehyde.*

By all accounts it was inspired by; *The Lamb lies down on Broadway – Genesis, Snow Goose – Camel* and *The Wall – Pink Floyd.* August company indeed but it is a worthy inclusion.

Divided into ten songs and book-ended by two epics it (actually) plays as one continuous track with recurring leitmotifs.

Dark and foreboding as befits the overall concept it does have its lighter moments albeit musically and not matching the lyrical content which is often apocalyptic in nature.

Vocals are, in the main, shared with *Valerie Gracious* who also plays piano. *Valerie* and *Phideaux* previously shared a stage for a school production of the biblical story of Moses. Her voice is best appreciated on *the doctrine of eternal ice (part two)* which also features the moog.

Unsurprisingly piano is the dominant instrument and flows beguilingly in front of the orchestra which is conducted by *Paul Rudolph.*

Overblown, pretentious retrospective and unoriginal are some of the accusations leveled but there is little merit to the accusations, and this stands up as one of the great progressive concept albums of the new century and reminiscent in style and grandeur to the UK's *Mandalaband.*

Thank you for the evil has a sinister feel and offers the lyric "lock down in the safety net, opiated by the television set" which is almost prophetic of the situation we find ourselves in circa 2020/21.

Although it forms part of a trilogy *Doomsday* easily stands alone as an album to 'enjoy' - in its own right.

Formaldehyde is the high point and not just for the inclusion of *Martin Orford. Stephen Dundon* (flute) and *Matthew Parmenter* (violin) are the other guests to appear on this track and their contributions are evident very early. Vocals are delivered in a folk style by *Valerie Gracious* and lush with counterpoint male 'pop' vocal.

Phideaux may have taken too long to round out the epic and in the interim *Doomsday* has become something of a collector's item.

Pink Floyd – Meddle (1971)

Pink Floyd had, arguably, three eras with *Syd Barrett, Roger Waters* and *David Gilmour* alternately leading the band. *Barrett's* tenure was relatively short in the scheme of things and often exhibited a psychedelic whimsy which was not embraced by too many. His legacy lived on and gave him the immortal status of 'legend'.

Roger Waters led the band to unprecedented success with several albums while *David Gilmour* took *Floyd* into new directions while maintaining the trademark sound.

Meddle proved a landmark on several levels after a couple of soundtrack albums which were not overly successful. Perhaps the most cohesive album to date consisting of six tracks with two seeming like material left-over from the whimsy *Barrett* era and included the superb epic title track.

One of these days opens the album and captivates the listener introducing one to the future sound which audiences would embrace to the full. Part of the vocal is almost a forerunner to the metal growl while showcasing *Gilmour's* trademark guitar.

A pillow of winds continues in similar fashion with superb sound effects and more guitar of the style fans were soon to become accustomed to.

Fearless includes the 'Liverpool anthem' otherwise known as 'You'll never walk alone' – a song written by *Rogers and Hammerstein* for the 1945 show *Carousel* and huge hit single for *Gerry and the Pacemakers* in 1963 before being adopted by the football club.

Side one on the original album was played out with *San Tropez* in an almost jazz club style with piano and strummed guitar. *Seamus* sounds as though they had time on their hands and were simply having a little fun. Footage of *Waters* encouraging the dog to whine, and bark can be viewed on the DVD *Live at Pompeii* (2003) although the original film circulated in British cinemas in the early seventies.

Side two featured the epic *Meddle* and has never aged sounding as good today and appreciated best through head-phones.

A slow builder which brought out the very best in *Richard Wright* (keyboards) and *Nick Mason* (drums). *Gilmour's* vocals and guitar playing are nothing short of amazing whilst *Waters* plays steady bass and adds effects.

For such a complex piece it was performed live a few times over the years and remains a fan favourite.

Waters was to take the band to great heights with the albums *Dark side of the Moon* (1973) and *The Wall* (1979).

Gilmour-led *Floyd* carried on after the break-up to the absolute disgust of *Waters* and a bitter feud was to ensue for many years until tentative 'peace' was restored.

A Momentary lapse of Reason (1987) remains the best from the 'Waterless" *Floyd*.

Meddle was a personal full-on introduction and an album which receives high rotation.

Porcupine Tree – In Absentia (2002)

Steven Wilson has proved himself time and again and is one of the most progressive musicians of the modern era in the full sense of the word. Never content to rest on his laurels he pushed boundaries with several projects before releasing superb solo albums but became the focus of some bizarre and unwarranted attention when he was considered to have strayed too far in the 'wrong direction'.

In Absentia is a term used in common law when a person is deemed mentally incapable of making their own decisions and decisions are made on their behalf. It is a Latin phrase meaning 'in absence'. Several songs on the album reflect the title and while not a concept album it does focus on a 'world-weary' view of the world in general.

Wilson was joined by *Gavin Harrison* (drums) with the album parts mostly decided upon prior to his arrival. *Richard Barbieri* (keyboards) and *Colin Edwin* (bass) made up the core band at this stage with a couple of backing vocalist performing on three tracks.

The first thing that is apparent is this is heavier bordering, at times, on prog/metal and a change of direction from the previous psychedelic styling. *Wilson* had rediscovered a passion for metal music and went on to work with *Opeth* among others and form some lasting friendships along the way.

Blackest Eyes was picked up for airplay by major league rock stations and received very well both critically and commercially and promoting the album to such a degree that it out-sold all previous albums.

It was re-issued a few years later in 5.1 surround and *Wilson* was to inhabit this medium by transferring older artists back catalogues to the same format, most notably from a personal perspective *Gentle Giant*.

The sound of Muzak is an incredible track and not overtly metal but heavier and harder-edged than previously. *Harrison* has become a renowned drummer in the progressive world and here he shines. The repeated chorus makes it memorable.

Gravity Eyelids is a song which lyrically reflects the album's title. *The creator has a mastertape* focuses on an unassuming man who eventually murders those around him – this is a reoccurring theme.

Collapse the light into Earth concludes the album on a sad and sombre note with lyrics one could easily attribute to *Roger Waters* and again reflect a sense of 'world weariness'.

Wedding Nails is purely instrumental and full of atmosphere while driving a hard-edged rock motif not unlike *Deep Purple*.

Wilson has given the pot a good stir on this album and repeated the dose with *Deadwing* (2005) – these two would sit comfortably as a double album.

Amazingly talented and diverse 'cherry picking' from his work over the years tends to leave one bewildered at the diversity and sheer musicianship of the man.

In Absentia rightly belongs high on the list of great albums from a great composer, musician, producer, mixer et al while he reignited interest in a genre which had been treading water.

Queensrÿche – Promised Land (1994)

With *Empire* (1990) *Queensrÿche* received unprecedented success and ultimately pressure to produce an album of similar or better quality. The single from that album *Silent Lucidity* propelled them into the mainstream but is not overtly representative of their style.

Progressive metal has reached saturation point but *Queensÿche* spearheaded the genre and remain relevant as the 21st century enters its third decade.

Promised Land is the American equivalent of the 'Great Aussie Dream'. Australians see the dream as owning their own home and being financially independent. *Promised Land* goes a little further in that the dream is to consume and own as many material possessions as possible.

Geoff Tate (vocal and keyboards), *Chris deGarmo* (guitars), *Michael Wilton* (guitar), *Eddie Jackson* (bass) and *Scott Rockenfield* (drums and percussion) were, at this juncture, *Queensrÿche*.

Opening track *9:28 A.M.* is collage of tape effects put together by *Scott Rockenfield* designed specifically for the album and make further appearances as the album unfolds.

It segues into *I Am I* full of heavy riffs with cello and sitar performed by *Chris DeGarmo* and rolls neatly into *Damaged* which is a (fairly) heavy rocker.

Out of my mind and *Bridge* are more acoustically based with the former bristling with superb bass playing from *Eddie Jackson* and some tasty saxophone which may be *Geoff Tate*.

The title track elevates the album to another level with a riff in '*Pink Floyd*' style circa *The Wall* (1979) but it's fleeting. A dark piece with more tape effects from

Rockenfield it also presents the best vocal performance from *Tate* and most assuredly it is his saxophone playing here. It ends with another *Floyd* moment with sound effects similar to '*Welcome to the Machine*' which flow seamlessly into *Disconnected* spelt phonetically as "*Dis cone nect ted*".

The song lives up its name and overtly progressive in nature. The drumming stands out but the whole thing is slightly marred by the repeated vocal line 'disconnected' being sung in a very pop fashion.

A ballad follows with *DeGarmo* playing some wonderfully sweet piano and *Tate* giving another great vocal performance. It appears to be an ode to the power and influence of television advertisements.

Both *My Global Mind* and *One More Time* are rocky with the latter more acoustic based.

Someone Else ends the album with mainly piano by *DeGarmo* and *Tate's* vocals. Not quite a ballad and given its striped-down nature it is very captivating and evocative. The song received a 'full band' performance on a subsequent re-issue in 2003 as a bonus track and, personally, detracts from the original version.

Other bonus tracks are *Real World* and two live cuts *Damaged* and *Real World* both taken from the same concert at London's Astoria Theatre on the 20th October 1994. There is much to like in *Queensrÿche's* varied catalogue, but *Promised Land* is a mature and well performed album presenting a band still coming to terms with greater adulation.

Riverside – Second Life Syndrome (2005)

Second full-length studio album from the Polish progressive metal band was to see their considerable profile elevated with a superb blend of modern prog and metal.

Mariusz Dudo (vocal and bass), *Piotr grundziński* (guitar), *Michał* Łapaj (keyboards) and *Piotr Kozieradzki* (drums) delivered the goods with a heavier sound than on their debut *'Out of myself'* (2003) turning up the metal sound but not abandoning the progressive and symphonic feel.

After the success of their debut the band was signed to heavy-weight label 'Inside Out' and, to date, remain with them. That speaks volumes.

Forming part of the dubbed *Reality Dream Trilogy* along with *Out of myself* and *Rapid Eye Movement* (2007) the album cemented their growing reputation within progressive and metal circles.

After is the opening track which does not jump out at one but begins slowly before a repetitive beat and backing vocal swirl around sounding dark and haunting, indeed the album (as a whole) has a similar feel throughout. It is not depressing by any means.

Volte-Face has some beautiful trademark guitar and a little metal style vocal here and there. Piano chimes in beautifully interwoven with sustained guitar notes and atmospheric keyboards.

Conceiving You picks up the pace with some stellar bass playing, superb guitar and 'rock-steady' drumming.

It is however the title track and epic (in three parts) which sets the album apart and also led many to make *'Pink Floyd'* comparisons (valid to a point) but *Riverside* are not mere copyists. That influence is only briefly displayed before the familiar sounds we have grown accustomed to break out with incredible affect. Other comparisons which have been made include *Tool* and *Porcupine Tree* and it does not stretch the imagination to see how some could extract their influence as this track continues.

Vocals and guitar are strong points with the band and are superb on *Second Life Syndrome Part Two* which segues into *Part Three* which is purely instrumental and somewhat experimental backed by pounding drums and understated bass.

There is not a single cut which does not fit on the album and *Artificial Smile, I turned you down* and *Reality Dream III* all continue the cohesion – which is evident with every single track – the latter of the three is sublime in its subtle delivery and fully instrumental.

Dance with the shadow is the second longest after the title track and is a slow builder. Beginning with beautiful atmospheric effects and an almost Irish folk feel to the vocal prior to *Piotr grundziński's* guitar drifting in then exploding in a virtuosic display of speed and dexterity, this track has it all. It concludes with the metal styling returning and vocals to match ending the track in a glorious crescendo.

Before is the final cut on the album leaving the overwhelming feeling that progressive music is in very good hands with *Riverside.*

Sadly, the death of *Piotr grundziński* in 2016 almost brought about their demise but to their credit the band was able to recover from that devastating blow and continue delivering the goods.

Piotr grundziński is best appreciated on the live album *Lost N Found – Live in Tilburg* (2017) especially on the accompanying DVD.

Sound of Contact – Dimensionaut (2013)

A concept album and brainchild of *Simon Collins* and *Dave Kerzner* this, sadly, proved to be the extent of their collaboration and a muted follow-up from *Sound of Contact* did not eventuate however all was not lost as *Dave Kerzner* went on to form *In Continuum* and carried the concept further with two amazingly good albums to date.

Collins (vocals, drums and percussion), *Kerzner* (keyboards, sound design and acoustic guitar) are joined by *Kelly Nordstrom* and *Matt Dorsey* both of whom play guitar and bass.

Let's get the obvious out of the way and deal with *Simon Collins* famous Father. Yes, he does play in a similar style and at times his voice bears a remarkable resemblance to his dad's (particularly on *Pale Blue Dot*) all of which should not detract from his abilities which are exceptional.

Conceptually concerning a space traveller looking to expand their horizons and experiences only to find that their home planet provides what they seek.

In essence it is progressive with pop sensibilities and the blend works exceedingly well as a cohesive whole. Some of the shorter songs have 'single' writ large but that would be to take them out of context, and they don't stand up to isolation from the album.

Starting with a radio signal as the antagonist is attempting to make a *Sound of Contact* prior to scaling the *Cosmic Distance Ladder* and looking back toward the Earth. The music to the opening two tracks is cinematic and expansive with the drumming coming fast and furious along with a wash of keyboards.

Pale Blue Dot is the first indication of the familial connection between *Phil* and *Simon Collins* with the vocals seemingly interchangeable such is the resemblance.

Following a series of songs in which our antagonist questions himself and his surroundings he appears to be at his wits end with '*Only breathing out*' questioning his own existence in the scheme of things. Thought provoking lyrics combined with atmospheric keyboards and pounding drum in the chorus make this a superb song which leads to further questioning of self as the next three tracks continue the self-assessment.

Mobius Slip is the epic final track in four parts and marks the first time the word 'continuum' appears and reasonably one can draw the conclusion that *Kerzner* used it for the next album to keep it cohesive.

Mobius Slip offers a progressive cinematic epic which leaves the concept 'up in the air' as the protagonist is resigned to the solidary existence, he has chosen but is equally filled with a sadness at the things he can no longer experience – the human touch.

Although the band no longer functions making this one and only release appear non-essential, I beg to differ. When *In Continuum* released their debut album it was quite clearly a follow-up which concludes with their second release therefore making an unlikely trilogy on a theme.

Simon Collins resides in Ireland and is quietly forging a solo career.

Spock's Beard – Beware of Darkness (1996)

Spock's Beard has a catalogue worth exploration, and this marked my introduction to the band making it influential on a personal level.

For many years *Neal Morse* was the driving force and *Spock's Beard* was a name taken from the Star Trek Vulcan character – played by Leonard Nimoy – who, in a later portrayal grew a beard!

Beware of Darkness is a *George Harrison* song which first appeared on his highly successful and triple vinyl solo album '*All things must pass*' (1970). *Morse* is quite honest in saying that he didn't know all the lyrics, and some are incorrect but his intention was to give the song 'the prog' treatment – he succeeded and listening to both versions back-to-back the differences are startling.

Thoughts – an amazing take on *Gentle Giant* with the harmonies that became synonymous with *Gentle Giant*. Interestingly, long after *Morse* had departed the band to pursue Christianity and then 'resurrect' his career as a solo artist and part of prog-super group *Transatlantic,* the song received an update in *After Thoughts* from the album *Brief Nocturnes and Dreamless Sleep* (2013).

The Doorway – second longest song on the album is keyboard driven with organ. It went on to be performed live on several occasions and is close to the best from the album. Lyrically it seems presumptuous and too easy to link with early religious feelings experienced by *Morse*.

Chatauqua – a short track of acoustic guitar in a *Steve Howe* style it is a beautiful interlude. It would be great to hear a duet for acoustic guitar performed by *Morse* and *Howe.*

Walking on the wind sounds a little like *Transatlantic* in the opening phases but that was in the future and offers an indication to *Morse's* input and impact on that band. It soon gives way to a grittier earthy sound of organ, guitar and drums before the main theme breaks in. The bass is notably high in the mix and sounds terrific. Alternating between quiet and frenzied passages this track is timeless and wonderful prog.

Waste Away is another acoustic guitar driven track and lyrically sparse with repeated lines and vocal refrain similar in style to *Yusef Islam* -formerly sixties pop idol *Cat Stevens*. This track too has pseudo-religious overtones.

Time has come – the epic final track begins with a seeming nod to *Gentle Giant* once again. The attack and punctuated staccato sounds are very similar to some of *GG's* early work.

This is a glorious track which in true epic tradition mines a number of differing styles with reoccurring riffs and tempo changes running the gauntlet from harmonic choral style singing to total rock workouts. Organ is very dominant and dramatic.

In essence *Beware of Darkness* embodies all that is good from progressive music and has stood the test of time – hard to believe it is celebrating its 25th anniversary as of 2021.

Chris Squire – Fish out of Water (1975)

Members of *YES* all tried their hand at solo projects with varying degrees of success. *Chris Squire* issued this amid a flurry activity from other members of the band and the band itself during some turbulent inter-band politics at the time.

This is in some way a tribute to the man who co-founded *YES* and became the main stay until his death. Composer, bassist, 12 string guitar, vocalist, arranger and producer for his solo project he gathered superb musicians to interpret his dream. *Bill Bruford, Mel Collins, Jimmy Hastings, Patrick Moraz, Barry Rose, Andrew Pryce Jackman* and an orchestra. Noteworthy is that *Pete Sinfield* is given credit for suggestions to *Safe*.

Hold out your hand opens with organ and bass which is so definitive of *Squire* that even should one be unaware of the artist it is evident from this opening sequence. Lyrically it is not the ambiguous psychedelically tinged words penned by *Jon Anderson* for his parent band.

You by my side a 'love song' with a difference – not the boy-meets-girl and falls in love type. The bass (as with most tracks) is all over this song and *Squire's* voice is unmistakable and easy to listen to.

Silently Falling is full of descending basslines and superb keyboards from *Patrick Moraz* – one time member of *YES* before *Rick Wakeman's* return to the fold. A more serious lyric is clear evidence of the talent of the man while the drumming of *Bill Bruford* is more akin with his work after his *YES* tenure.

Lucky Seven was released as a single to promote the album but (as is often the case) was 'mercilessly' edited and is therefore best enjoyed in its natural setting.

Safe (Canon Song) is the epic closing track and utilises the orchestra to the full with amazing bass accompanying the strings throughout. It builds powerfully, swirling in pseudo-classical style with horns prominent and adding to the grandeur. Lyrically the song to which *Sinfield* offered 'suggestions' which becomes evident in lines such as "When you face the doors of doubt" sounding like some unused *King Crimson* lyric. *Mel Collins* on saxophone is, predictably, a wonderful asset to anyone's album.

This monumental track ends with the music slowing down considerably and drifting toward the end gloriously.

Chris Squire's legacy with *YES* is immeasurable but his work outside the band is deserving of greater attention and *Fish out of Water* is not just a brilliant and timeless album but, in my opinion, the best solo album from any member of *YES*.

He also teamed-up with *Steve Hackett* in *Squackett* for the album *A life within a day* (2012) and worked with *Billy Sherwood* in *Conspiracy* who released two albums (*Conspiracy* (2000) and *The Unknown* (2003)).

Working with *Jimmy Page* and *Robert Planet* on an unrealised project *XYZ (ex-Yes and Zeppelin)* before recruiting *Trevor Horn* and *Geoffrey Downes (The Buggles)* he was instrumental in re-igniting *YES* with the album *Drama* (1980)

R.I.P. *Christopher Russell Edward Squire* (1948–2015)

Supertramp – Crime of the Century (1974)

Difficult for some to imagine the impact of this album, not just on a commercial and critical level, but on the future direction of a band who had, in all honesty, struggled to find a winning formula.

Roger Hodgson (vocal, guitar and piano) *Richard Davies* (vocal, keyboards) *John Helliwell* (saxophone and clarinet) *Doug Thomson* (bass) and *Bob Benberg* (drums and percussion) took the world by storm with *Supertramp's* third studio album with one being fortunate enough to see it performed in its entirety at the 1975 Reading Festival.

The album art had a grill suspended in the night sky with a pair of hands grabbing two bars – maybe a pictorial reference for their need to escape the mundane.

School opens with harmonica by *Richard Davies* prior the sound of school children playing in the yard then that shrill scream which still sends shivers down the spine. Memorable and unforgettable it drew one into an album a world apart from previous efforts.

Bloody well right saw release as the B side of the single *Dreamer* and received high rotation in the US from album-friendly rock stations lifting their profile immensely.

Hide in your shell makes even greater strides to the more progressive sound the band would embrace for a few highly successful years. Whispered opening vocals with piano give way to the sudden 'click' into heavier and rockier mode with the 'soon-to-be' trademark vocal harmonies. What used to be called the 'middle eight' has the song careening in a totally different direction with counter-point vocal exhibiting the high and low vocals.

Asylum is an amusing song with a deeper meaning. Listening to it years later it is immediately dated lyrically when the protagonist asks for 15 pence for cigarettes! The band may have been listening to *Pink Floyd's Dark side of the Moon* (1973) as the connotations are similar.

Rudy takes a philosophical look at a loner on a "train to nowhere". Again it paints a picture of a loner who is encouraged to take control but sadly ends up back on the train.

If everyone was listening appears to head in the same direction but this time concerns an actor who pleads that the curtain is not brought down to end the play. Musically it displays all the trademarks associated with *Supertramp* during their high-profile years.

The album concludes with the title track. The piano takes a lead role as the song builds. Together with the bass it makes it one of the most memorable on the album. Lead guitar swathes rush in and out as the song reaches its crescendo with plaintive piano chords and orchestral sounds. The most progressive leaning track it was a pointer to some of concluding songs featured on subsequent albums.

Supertramp never looked back and although their flower wilted somewhat, they have left a body of work which will live on.

The Tangent – Comm (2011)

Andy Tillison has steered *the Tangent* in various directions over the years, but this was one's doorway and still an album which brings delight.

Tillison (keyboards and vocal), *Jonathan Barrett* (bass), *Luke Machin* (guitar), *Nick Rickwood* (drums) and *Theo Travis* (saxophone and flute) perform on the album although the drums in live performance at the time were played by *Tony Latham*.

The Wiki man the opening epic sets out their stall to deliver an album conceptually based on communication both old and new and as the title clearly indicates this one is modern.

Tillison's lyrics can be bitingly sarcastic and often stray into the political arena. Here he looks into the persona of those who seem to depend on their computer and communication modes to 'survive' the modern world. He refers to it all as "strange days" as the 'keyboard warriors' pen, mostly, other people's thoughts. Musically captivating, lyrically humours and wittingly biting it is a track which invites revisiting.

The Mind's Eye and *Shoot them down* appear to drift from the overall theme but offer a glimpse of times gone by in the grime of northern English cities. At times it feels slightly autobiographical in nature with references to recitals and sonatas.

Tech Support Guy is a hilarious look at the myriad of potential problems that this individual may encounter all of which are happening on the same day. They've lost their network and the server's down and they all just blame 'Adam'.

Titanic calls Carpatha is used as a metaphor for a number of situations over the years to highlight how communication has changed but modern technology isn't always the answer.

Carpatha received the first ever SOS call from the Titanic in April 1912 but the distance between both vessels meant they arrived too late to prevent a heavy loss of life. In total contrast the Apollo 13's disaster which happened in 1971 200,000 miles from Earth was saved by a simple 2-way radio system.

Tillison's further observations are illuminating and even though we think we are aware of the impact of modern technology and communications the quotes used in the CD booklet enable us to 're-think' what we thought we knew.

As of the time of the album's recording some 500 million users log in to Facebook on any given day with an average of 130 "friends". By 2011 campaigns on Facebook actually brought down governments in Magreb and Arabia!

It is all set to superb progressive music but that should never detract from the underlying message.

Two bonus tracks adorn the 'limited edition' album *the spirit of the Net* which is in keeping with the overall theme but not as strong as the preceding songs. The other is a live recording of the *Genesis* song *Watcher of the skies* from *Foxtrot* (1972). It is interesting but the recording is a little 'muddy' and easily forgotten about once the novelty of hearing how they performed it is over.

The Tangent have released several great albums since *Comm* but for the epic closing track alone it is one that keeps bringing me back.

Transatlantic – The Whirlwind (2009)

Are *Transatlantic* a super-group? Perhaps an over-used term but when musicians of this caliber and pedigree come together then the expectancy is high.

Neal Morse had been the driving force behind *Spock's Beard* and plays; keyboards, acoustic guitar, percussion and vocals. *Mike Portnoy Dream Theater* drummer and sometime vocalist has since played in a few other projects which befits his status as 'workaholic'. *Roine Stolt* is credited on the album with; electric guitars, vocals, percussion and additional mellotron, minimoog and soundscapes (any and) all he has utilised in his parent band *Flower Kings*. *Pete Trewavas* on bass, vocals, synth and orchestration is currently a full-time member of *Marillion* since replacing *Diz Minnitt* in 1982.

Their collective CVs would fill several pages and their individual bodies of work perform an equal task. Unlike many 'super-groups' they really do live up to the hype and on their third album delivered to the absolute maximum – as good as the other two albums are.

The Whirlwind is broken into twelve sections with a total running time of almost 78 minutes. It plays as one continuous piece of music (which may seem obvious) and should be enjoyed as such, but the sections enable one to highlight which part of the album is being discussed.

Overture/Whirlwind is, as the title suggests, classical in approach prior to the vocal section with themes reoccurring throughout, not just this section but theentire work.

The section titled '*On the Prowl*' is almost a showcase for *Trewavas's* bass and one is at loss to recall any *Marillion* album where he sounded this good – I'm sure he did, maybe it's the mix.

Out of the Night as the main theme returns with the vocal of *Morse* strong and intense and the best outside early *Spock's Beard* heard in years the band seem at ease with one another displaying a 'band feel' more apparent than on their first two albums.

Evermore – is a marvelous section with *Portnoy's* drumming coming to the fore and lead guitar playing staccato style while *Stolt* takes lead vocal, his unmistakable voice leading the song with pace and polish as it segues into 'Set us Free' again returning to the main theme with a jazzy feel to the keyboards.

Lay down your life is the most dramatic section aside the *Overture* and the *Whirlwind* reprise. It has echoes of *YES* at their best with all four musicians displaying their credentials to the full.

'Is it really happening?' is a slow building section which begins with effects and atmospheric ambience before sliding into a steady and repetitive throbbing bassline with (almost) chanted vocal parts. As it reaches its climax the *Genesis* style keyboards send the music madly rushing to a conclusion.

Dancing with eternal glory/Whirlwind (Reprise) breaks in with piano and voice and some beautiful, understated guitar. A lengthy section which concludes the album in the manner it began.

Transatlantic have released five studio albums to date with 'Whirlwind' being the most cohesive and best. A few live albums also exist but for my part this album is the apex of their output.

Unitopia – Artificial (2010)

Sean Timms and *Mark Trueack* were the driving force behind Adelaide's *Unitopia* and had a friendship which thrived prior to their founding the band. It was the bands penultimate studio album.

Artificial is also known as *Artificial Suite* and is a concept played out to a back-drop of crossover progressive rock, jazz, folk and world music and highlighting some of their influences to great effect.

Trueack (vocals) and *Timms* (keyboards) are joined by *Matt Williams* (guitars), *Shaun Duncan* (basses), *Jamie Jones* (drums) with *Tim Irrgang* (assorted percussion) and *Peter Raidel* (saxophones). The album also boasts several guest musicians making for a grand orchestral sound.

Suffocation segues into the *Artificial World* with a lament to our world and its decline on many levels but mainly the simplicity of days gone by when people appeared to have more time for each other and communicated without the aid of modern technology.

Nothing last forever references the *Beatles* and a sound not unlike their later work with some *ELO* overlap. A couple of *Beatles* songs (*Come Together* and *Fool on the Hill*) are incorporated into the lyric with "maybe the boys from Liverpool got it right".

Tesla is an epic track which clearly indicates the virtuosity of *Timms* and the voice of *Trueack* although every member of the extended band get their moment in the sun.

Reflections displays a certain *Genesis* feel to it with the keyboards and the vocal reminding one of *Tony Banks* and *Peter Gabriel* without appearing mere copyist.

The Power of 3 segues into *Rule of 3* and are absolute stand-outs and extremely symphonic in nature with all those string players realising the music of *Timms* and *Trueack* to the full. Saxophone is beautiful and jazzy.

Gone in the blink of an eye – exhibits incredible 3- or 4-part harmonies again lamenting loss but more people's preoccupation with the "moment" without appreciating what they have before it is all gone 'in the blink of an eye'. The jazzy saxophone licks remain to the end of the track.

The Great Reward concludes the suite with positive encouragement to see the bigger picture while reprising the main theme and '*Nothing lasts forever*'.

A superb album of timeless music and heartfelt message but *Unitopia* soon imploded, and *Sean Timms* went on to form *Southern Empire* while *Mark Trueack* formed *United Progressive Fraternity*.

Southern Empire have released two fine albums which veer more toward the heavier end of progressive rock while *United Progressive Fraternity* have become a vehicle for *Trueack's* passion and concern for the planet and its myriad of problems – mostly 'man-made'. He draws in many like-minded musicians from the world of 'prog' – most notably *Steve Hackett* – while expanding his relationship with *Steve Unruh* who has worked with *Resistor* and *Samurai of Prog* among others as well as releasing solo material.

The Who – Quadrophenia (1973)

A concept which is much more satisfying than *Tommy* (1969) even though the latter receives greater attention from (in particular) *Pete Townshend*. A simple story surrounding the world of the 'mods' and one individual's exploits from out-of-work and domestically out-of-favour from his home to the shores of Brighton on England's south coast.

An album on which *John Entwhistle* shines – exhibiting his mastery on bass guitar as well as horns – his first instrument. *Roger Daltrey's* vocals never sounded better. *Keith Moon* is more subdued than usual but 'let loose' now and then however overall, his drumming is controlled and the better for that. *Pete Townshend* does what he does best writing and producing this concept while being one of the world's most under-rated but brilliant guitarists. Collectively the *Who* gelled so well together even though they were often, personally at loggerheads.

I am the Sea incorporates the four main reoccurring themes from the album into an 'overture' with the band displaying progressive sensibilities for which they seldom received acknowledgement. The grandeur is amazing and gets the whole venture off to a wonderful start.

The real me has our protagonist questioning his metal stability and visiting the doctor to elicit help. When he tells his mother that he's crazy she tells him that she knows how it feels because it "runs in the family".

There is not much 'mod' terminology used save *I'm one* but the whole mod culture is alluded to in the style of dress and drug of choice.

I've had enough contains some wonderful harmonies between *Daltrey* and *Townshend* and marks a dimension seldom if ever written about but one which the pair indulged in regularly with *Entwhistle* sometimes contributing.

5:15 reprises *'Cut my hair'* and contains sound effects of the south coast bound train speeding into a tunnel blowing its horn. Vocally it is performed in a call and response mode.

Keith Moon takes the vocal limelight in *Bell Boy* and he played it to the hilt. Delivered in an exaggerated cockney accent it did nonetheless suit his limited vocal range and out-of-tune style.

Doctor Jimmy projects the growing mental demise of our protagonist as he clearly exhibits a Jekyll and Hyde persona. Brutal and misogynistic with a reprise of the main theme in *'is it me?'*

Love reign o-er me or *Pete's theme* ends the album as it began with an element of overture as various themes come and go and *Daltrey's* vocals range from passionate to full-blooded.

A concept album often over-looked amid the plethora of concepts released around the same time may have been due to its being reality based and not a phantasmagorical journey to other worlds.

The Who has enjoyed a longevity which is not reflected in the number of albums released over the years – some brilliant, some not so.

Quadrophenia remains as relevant today even though the mod culture is no longer in vogue and others have come and gone since. The message of feeling alienated from society and mental instability are still with us – as are the *Who*.

YES – Close to the Edge (1972)

Often cited as the greatest example of early symphonic progressive music *Close to the Edge* has never gone out of fashion and retains itself in the hearts of fans old and new. Some will attest to it being THE greatest prog album of all time and many list it highly in their top ten. Either way, its impact was incredible and its durability amazing. To present an album with just three songs – one side-long and two on the other side of the original vinyl was astonishing at the time.

Jon Anderson (vocals), *Steve Howe* (guitars), *Rick Wakeman* (keyboards), *Chris Squire* (bass) and *Bill Bruford* (percussion) have gone into 'YES' folklore as the classic line-up. They possessed a chemistry which is undeniable and for a short period of time in the long career of the band enjoyed a critical and financial success previously unobtainable.

Close to the Edge has received a great deal of attention over the years and again makes a splash in any poll for best prog epic ever. There is little doubt of its importance particularly in the first wave of progressive rock.

Split into four sections it has been dissected by some prominent musicians and musicologists including a classical aficionado who regularly posts his views on the 'daily Doug'. His comments as he stop/starts his chosen album or track are insightful and he is often heard to say, "listen to that bass" or "they can't do that!" while reading the lyric sheet with amazement at the profundity.

The segment *I get up I get down* from the title track will often be cited as *Jon Anderson* greatest vocal moment. Just when you think his range has been tested to the limit, he raises the bar again. He formed a formidable singing partnership with *Chris Squire* who was infatuated with choral or church music and sang in a church choir. That partnership was pivotal to this album as a whole and (in particular) the title track.

And you and I is another track split into four segments and one which became a concert favourite for years to follow.

The main theme returns often but the segments are much easier to recognize in their distinctness.

Individually each band member has a chance to shine, and *Rick Wakeman's* footprint is all over the album. His array of keyboards was breath-taking and his mastery of them unbelievable. Likewise *Steve Howe* plays with the passion and pseudo-classical style which *YES* fans have long adored. *Bill Bruford* has a wonderful jazz feel to his playing and certainly never considered his style rock. Finally the irrepressible *Chris Squire* squeezes every last nuance from his Rickenbacker bass – an instrument with which he became synonymous.

Siberian Khatru – even *Anderson* had no idea what *Khatru* meant but has revealed that he sought out the meaning and was informed it is of Arabic extraction and means "as you wish".

Another song to transfer to the live arena it has appeared on many of their live albums since – and there are a lot of live albums!

In summary *Close to the Edge* shaped and changed the musical landscape and the mindset of what was possible. Many feel *YES* took the whole concept to extremes and cite *Tales from topographic oceans* (1973) as a prime example.

I happen to disagree but that's a story for another day.

YES – Keystudio (2001)

These are studio tracks taken from the two *Keys to Ascension* live albums released in 1996/97. Essentially, they were to entice fans into buying yet another live album. The amount of live product over the years would out-strip some artists entire studio output. The two albums were taken from one concert and the decision made to market them separately with both having added studio tracks. What made it essential for many die-hard fans was that both *Wakeman* and *Howe* had rejoined *Anderson, Squire* and *White* after the departure of *Kaye* and *Rabin*. The history of *YES* overflows with comings and goings and *Wakeman* was to depart once more replaced by *Billy Sherwood* who produced this album.

This is both a solid album and wonderful idea but is often overlooked in the *YES* canon. It barely was reviewed by music press and did not trouble any chart compiler – anywhere! The seven tracks are all lengthy with a combined duration in excess of 74 minutes. That's real value.

Wakeman and *Howe* both expressed concerns that the new studio material should stand alone as it proved the best for a long time and a long time since this version of *YES* produced any music together.

Foot Prints opens a cappella but soon gives way to the entire band in full cry and sounding very good indeed.

Be the one – was recorded start to finish in one take according to *Chris Squire* that had not happened for a considerable amount of time. This is vintage *YES*, with the (added) bonus of modern technology to bring out the richness of their sound.

Mind Drive is the first of two epics on the album beginning life with a *Squire* riff with *White* and guitarist *Jimmy Page* during the sessions for the proposed *XYZ* project. *Howe* is at his very best with trademark guitar soaring in and out throughout including in Spanish style. Bass is excellent and vocals amazing. *White's* drumming is heavy and in full rock mode. Keyboards add all the subtle touches and more. This alone makes it an album which deserved a better reception.

Bring me power is credited to *Anderson/Howe* and that also had not happened since the late seventies.

Sign Language is the shortest and only instrumental track. Building slowly, it is a beautiful sound reminiscent of 'classic *YES*' with superb orchestration.

That, that is – an epic which was taken from the first *KTA* live album was eagerly anticipated by fans when the news got out concerning the "reunion" of the classic line-up, except of course *White* was in place of *Bruford* and has occupied that position since the latter's departure – still there to this day. His drumming on this track is innovative on a very dynamically shifting song.

'*Children of the Light*' is slightly different from the version issued on *KTA2*. Firstly, the title is '*Children of Light*'. Secondly the keyboard introduction was added or had been omitted from the *KTA2* version. Lastly the lyrics have been tweaked a little.

This is a remarkable album and why it failed commercially is difficult to fathom. Perhaps the time between recording and release when the band had changed configuration again had something to do with it.

It rightly deserves a place in the very best albums from *YES* and there have been plenty over the years.

www.ingramcontent.com/pod-product-compliance
Lightning Source LLC
Chambersburg PA
CBHW031055250726
48655CB00004B/1444